Quick After-Work

EGETARIAN COOKBOOK

JUDY RIDGWAY

FISHER
er
BOOKS™

Publishers: Bill Fisher
Howard Fisher
Helen V. Fisher

North American   Helen V. Fisher
Editors: Sarah Smith

Cover Design: FifthStreet*design*
Book Design: Josh Young
Illustrations: Madeleine David
Book Production: Deanie Wood

Some photographs courtesy of U.S. Quality Bean Information Bureau, The British Egg Information Bureau, and Food and Wine from France. Photographs opposite pages 41 and 137 by Martin Brigdale.

First published in Great Britain in 1994 by Piatkus Books, London Copyright © 1994 Judy Ridgway The moral right of the author has been asserted.

North American Edition Published by Fisher Books 4239 W. Ina Road, Suite #101 Tucson, AZ 85741 (520) 744-6110

© 1996 Fisher Books
Printed in USA
Printing 10 9 8 7 6 5 4 3 2 1

Library of Congress
Cataloging-in-Publication Data

Ridgway, Judy.
    Quick after-work vegetarian cookbook / Judy Ridgway.
      p. cm.
   Includes index.
   ISBN 1-55561-090-0 (pb)
    1. Vegetarian cookery. 2. Quick and easy cookery. I. Title.
TX837.R486 1996
641.5' 636—dc20   96-2432
                         CIP

Nutrient analysis was calculated using The Food Processor® for Windows software program, version 6.0, copyright 1987-1995 by ESHA Research.

    Analysis does not include optional ingredients or variations. Where an ingredient amount is a range, the higher number is used.

    The following abbreviations are used:
      Cal = Calories
      Prot = Protein
      Carb = Carbohydrates
      Fib = Fiber
      Tot. Fat = Total Fat
      Sat. Fat = Saturated Fat
      Chol = Cholesterol

Notice: The information in this book is true and complete to the best of our knowledge. The information in this book is general and is offered with no guarantees on the part of the author or Fisher Books. The author and publisher disclaim all liability in connection with use of this book.

CH   7/97

Contents

INTRODUCTION

Instead of having more leisure time in the 1990s I seem to have less! I am lucky to be working, but, like nearly everyone else I know, I am working longer hours and coming home later. Once home I just want to flop down in front of the television or, on more energetic evenings, attend classes, concerts or sports events.

What I don't want to do is spend a lot of time—or my remaining energy—slaving away in the kitchen. I need easy yet attractive meals that can be prepared in half an hour or so. This is not as unrealistic as it might sound. I have spent months working on recipes and menus that fulfill these criteria and this book is the result of that work.

Some people think that vegetarian food takes longer to prepare than "meat and two veg" but you'll see that this is just not true. All the recipes in the book can be prepared in about half an hour, and many are ready to eat in even less time.

Although I sometimes cook the whole evening meal from ingredients bought that day, more often I mix fresh ingredients with canned, bottled or frozen foods that I have on hand. A really interesting stock of ingredients can help considerably in turning readily available everyday food into a real feast.

I am fortunate to have a variety of ethnic and specialty stores in my neighborhood, but wherever I am, I never pass an interesting food shop without looking for things to add to my store. I recently purchased a jar of grilled and marinated baby onions in olive oil, some capers and a large bottle of pickled lemons from Spain—I'm still learning how to use the lemons to best advantage.

My pantry also contains a wide selection of basics so that I never get bored with the same type of pasta, and I can substitute couscous, bulgar or polenta for rice whenever I feel like it. There are also plenty of dried and canned beans and peas and a selection of nuts and seeds. I have given suggestions for what to keep in your pantry on page 7.

Deciding on the menu for the evening takes just a minute or two and is inspired either by the contents of the pantry or my vegetable bin, or by the fruit and vegetables on sale at roadside stands, markets and supermarkets on the way to and from my office. Some of the two-course combinations developed during the testing of this book are given on page 8.

I usually use fresh herbs, and have done so for all the recipes in this book, except where stated. The dishes are intended to serve four, but as appetites vary you may find they will feed more or fewer people. Throughout the book, recipes suitable for vegans are marked with a Ⓥ.

I do hope this book will encourage everyone who has to produce quick after-work meals to experiment with different ingredients and only use the supermarket freezer in an emergency!

EATING A BALANCED DIET

There is no reason why a diet free from meat and fish should not be as healthy and nutritious as any other. All the nutrients you need can easily be obtained from vegetarian foods. Indeed, vegetarians are better placed than most to follow today's healthy-eating guidelines.

As long as you do not rely too heavily on dairy products, there is very little saturated fat. The diet is naturally rich in carbohydrate foods such as pasta, bread, potatoes, beans and lentils. There are also plenty of protein-rich vegetables such as dried and canned beans, nuts and seeds, rice, bread, pasta and oatmeal.

When protein foods are eaten together you gain even more protein than if you eat them separately. One of the best combinations is cereals or grains and beans or legumes. Examples include baked beans on toast, hummus with pita bread, rice cooked with beans, peanut butter sandwiches and taco shells filled with lentils or refried beans. These combinations are particularly important for vegans who do not eat eggs or cheese.

A vegetarian diet should also be rich in fresh fruit and vegetables to ensure that you get needed vitamins and minerals. It is important to remember that iron from vegetable sources is more effectively absorbed in the presence of vitamin C. Good combinations here include toast and orange juice at breakfast and watercress-and-orange salad with other meals.

Vegans may need to think about giving their children more calcium-rich foods such as almonds, sesame seeds, whole-wheat bread, fresh greens and vitamin-B12-enriched soy milk or breakfast cereals.

The easiest way to eat a balanced diet is to eat as many different kinds of food as possible. Experiment with unusual cereals such as polenta (yellow cornmeal), couscous, bulgar and quinoa as well as with soy products like tofu, miso and tempeh. Try brewer's yeast, seaweed and tahini paste. Mix all of these with everyday items such as potatoes, bread, cheese, carrots, apples and oranges.

If you regularly grab a quick snack or prepare the whole meal in half an hour, try to do something different every day. Do not rely on just a small number of tried and trusted dishes. The more you experiment the wider your range will become and the more nutritious your meals will be.

VEGETARIAN CHEESE

An increasing number of cheeses are being made with vegetarian coagulants of various kinds. There are rennet-free versions of most of the traditional cheeses and some of the European classics. In addition, many of the new soft cheeses are made without rennet. If the cheese is not labeled or you are not sure how it is made, buy only from a cheese specialist who can tell you all you need to know about each cheesemaker's production methods.

THE PANTRY

BASIC INGREDIENTS

These staple ingredients form the base of many quick after-work meals:

- Long pasta - spaghetti, spaghettini and fettucine
- Pasta shapes - bows, fusilli and rigatoni
- Chinese egg noodles and Japanese buckwheat noodles
- Rice - basmati, long-grain and risotto
- Quick-cook polenta (yellow cornmeal)
- Bulgur
- Couscous
- Canned kidney or cannellini beans and chickpeas or garbanzos
- Dried lentils and beans
- Canned tomatoes and tomato purée
- Frozen peas, corn and asparagus
- Vegetable stock cubes and brewer's yeast
- Soy and Tabasco® sauces
- Sunflower and olive oils

INTERESTING FLAVORING INGREDIENTS

I use these items for inspiration and to add interest to dishes:

- A variety of herbs and spices
- Dried wild mushrooms
- Sun-dried tomatoes - packed in oil, dry and paste
- Pesto sauce
- Horseradish sauce
- Green and black olives - whole and paste
- Capers
- Peanut butter
- Flaked almonds and pine nuts
- Sunflower, sesame and pumpkin seeds
- Chinese black-bean sauce
- Chinese plum sauce
- Vegetarian Worcestershire sauce
- Sesame oils, plain and toasted
- Curry powder
- Sherry and balsamic vinegars

MENU SUGGESTIONS

Here are some combinations for quick meals. The desserts are up to you.
(Ⓥ = suitable for vegans)

Celeriac-and-Carrot Soup Ⓥ
Tomatoes Stuffed with Mushrooms Ⓥ
Spicy Corn Pilaf / Banana Kebabs Ⓥ

Leek-and-Walnut Omelet
Chickpeas with Spinach Ⓥ
Classic Welsh Rarebit

Brie-and-Onion Soup
Orange-and-Date Salad Ⓥ
Flour tortillas

Avocado Salad with Hot Grapefruit Sauce
Polenta Rustica
Zucchini Salad Ⓥ

Eggplant-and-Mozzarella Bruschetta
Bean-and-Celery Soup Ⓥ
Watercress-and-Pistachio Salad Ⓥ

Warm Carrot Salad with Arugula Ⓥ
Eggplant with Olive Paste and Tomatoes Ⓥ
Liptauer Cheese / sweet-and-sour pickles

Chilled Beet-and-Orange Soup
Pasta Bows with Goat-Cheese Sauce
Zucchini-and-Dill Molded Salad Ⓥ

Tofu-and-Watercress Pâté with toast Ⓥ
Lentil Burgers / Beans Provençale Ⓥ
Apple-Date-and-Endive Salad Ⓥ

Red-Pepper Salad Ⓥ
Egyptian Rice / Falafel Ⓥ
Egg Pots Provençale

Chapter One

SOUPS

Soups make a very good start to a meal but I used to think that it was necessary to cook them for a long time to concentrate the flavor, so they rarely appeared on my table during the week. However, while testing recipes for this book I discovered that quite the opposite is true. With the right ingredients, well-flavored soups can be produced in a short time.

Some of the hot soups, such as Tuscan Soup with Pasta, are thick and filling and can easily be turned into a main course by serving them accompanied by whole-grain bread. You might also add rice, noodles or bulgur to the soup.

Cold soups are attractive in hot weather, but if the meal has to be ready in half an hour there is no time to chill a cooked soup. The answer is to make soups that do not need to be cooked, using fruit and vegetables such as melon, cucumber and tomatoes. You will also benefit from the higher vitamin content.

When you have a little time to spare make a double quantity of any of these soups. With the exception of Stracciatella, they all freeze well. On another occasion you will then have a ready-prepared first course to help you to prepare a full meal even faster.

VEGETABLE STOCK Ⓥ

Keep this flavorful stock on hand for use in your home-made soups and in any recipe calling for stock or broth.

1 garlic clove, minced
1 onion, peeled and chopped
1 celery stalk, chopped
2 carrots, peeled and sliced
1 zucchini, peeled and sliced
1/4 cup (60ml) chopped fresh
  parsley
1 parsnip, peeled and sliced
10 cups water

1. Combine all ingredients in a large pot. Simmer, covered, 45 minutes.
2. Strain broth.

Makes 2 quarts stock.

1 cup contains:

| | | | | Tot. | Sat. | | |
Cal	Prot	Carb	Fib	Fat	Fat	Chol	Sodium
29	1g	7g	2g	0g	0g	0mg	13mg

CELERIAC-AND-CARROT SOUP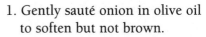

These two root vegetables work well together to produce a sweet and velvety soup. There is no need for any extra herbs or spices. Just use a good extra-virgin olive oil and fresh vegetables.

1 small onion, peeled and chopped
2 tablespoons extra-virgin olive oil
3/4 lb. (340g) celeriac or celery root, peeled and chopped
3 large carrots, peeled and chopped
Salt and pepper to taste
3-4 cups (750-1000ml) vegetable stock, page 10

1. Gently sauté onion in olive oil to soften but not brown.
2. Add celeriac or celery root and carrots and cook, stirring constantly, 3-4 minutes.
3. Add salt, pepper and stock and bring to a boil. Cover and reduce heat. Simmer 15-20 minutes until vegetables are tender.
4. Purée in a blender or food processor or rub through a sieve. Reheat and serve.

Makes 4 servings.

Each serving contains:

Cal	Prot	Carb	Fib	Tot. Fat	Sat. Fat	Chol	Sodium
136	2g	18g	6g	7g	1g	0mg	149mg

CILANTRO-AND-CHILE POTATO SOUP ⓥ

An excellent produce store near my apartment always has mountains of fresh, green cilantro (coriander) leaves and I have become addicted to their spicy flavor. I have used them in this simple potato soup to give an interesting twist.

2 cloves garlic, peeled and sliced

1 onion, peeled and sliced

1 tablespoon olive oil

1 can (8-oz. / 225g) tomatoes

1-1/2 lb. (700g) potatoes, peeled and diced

3 cups (750ml) vegetable stock, page 10, or water

Pinch of dried oregano

1 whole small green chile pepper

Salt and pepper to taste

1/4 cup (60ml) chopped fresh cilantro or coriander leaves

Juice of 1/2 lemon

1. In a saucepan, sauté garlic and onion in olive oil 4-5 minutes to brown lightly.

2. Add tomatoes and their juice, potatoes, stock or water, oregano, chile pepper, salt, pepper and 1 tablespoon of the cilantro or coriander.

3. Bring to a boil. Cover and simmer 15-20 minutes until potatoes are cooked.

4. Remove chile pepper. Spoon soup into bowls and sprinkle with lemon juice and remaining cilantro or coriander.

Makes 4 servings.

Each serving contains:

Cal	Prot	Carb	Fib	Tot. Fat	Sat. Fat	Chol	Sodium
213	4g	43g	5g	4g	1g	0mg	180mg

TUSCAN SOUP WITH PASTA ⓥ

This thick, heart-warming soup is from Poggi Bonzi in the Chianti Classico area of Tuscany. The locals pour it over thick chunks of country bread and then drizzle extra-virgin olive oil over all.

1 can (14-oz. / 400g) chickpeas or garbanzos, drained

1 can (14-oz. / 400g) chopped tomatoes

3 cups (750ml) vegetable stock, page 10

1 clove garlic, crushed

1/4 cup (60ml) extra-virgin olive oil, plus more to serve

1/4 teaspoon dried rosemary

1 tablespoon tomato purée

Freshly ground black pepper

2 oz. (60g) soup pasta

1. Purée chickpeas or garbanzos and tomatoes and juice in a blender or food processor. Stir in stock.

2. Gently sauté garlic in olive oil 1-2 minutes. Do not allow it to brown. Add puréed vegetables, rosemary, tomato purée and pepper.

3. Bring to a boil and simmer 5 minutes. Add pasta and cook another 10 minutes. Serve with extra-virgin olive oil.

Makes 4 servings.

Each serving contains:

Cal	Prot	Carb	Fib	Tot. Fat	Sat. Fat	Chol	Sodium
350	11g	42g	7g	17g	2g	0mg	196mg

BEAN-AND-CELERY SOUP Ⓥ

This is another soup typical of central Tuscany. No herbs are added because the soup gets its flavor from the olive oil; so buy the best extra-virgin oil you can afford.

1 small onion, peeled and sliced

1-1/2 cups sliced celery

2 tablespoons extra-virgin olive oil, plus extra for serving

1 cup (200g) red kidney beans, drained

3 cups (750ml) vegetable stock, page 10

Salt and pepper to taste

1. Gently sauté onion and celery in olive oil for 4-5 minutes until vegetables start to soften. Do not allow them to become too brown.

2. Add remaining ingredients and bring to a boil. Cover and simmer 20 minutes.

3. You can serve the soup as is or purée it in a food processor or blender, then reheat. Offer more extra-virgin olive oil for diners to add to their soup.

Makes 4 servings.

Each serving contains:

Cal	Prot	Carb	Fib	Tot. Fat	Sat. Fat	Chol	Sodium
155	5g	19g	6g	7g	1g	0mg	118mg

BRUSSELS SPROUTS SOUP Ⓥ

Sprouts are widely available throughout the winter but they are rarely used in soups. This seems rather a pity when their flavor is so popular. I have made this soup both with and without the chestnuts and I cannot make up my mind which I prefer! Try it both ways and make your own decision. If you are not using the chestnuts, reduce stock by 3/4 to 1 cup (185-250ml).

1 large onion, peeled and chopped

1 tablespoon cooking oil

1 teaspoon butter (optional)

1/4 cup (60ml) sherry

1 lb. (450g) Brussels sprouts, trimmed and quartered

3 cups (750ml) vegetable stock, page 10

Salt and pepper to taste

1 can (6-oz. / 175g) chestnuts, drained (optional)

1/4 cup (60ml) half-and-half (optional)

1. Gently sauté onion in oil and butter, if using, for 4-5 minutes until onion starts to soften. Do not allow it to brown.

2. Add sherry and bring to a boil. Add Brussels sprouts, stock, salt, pepper and chestnuts, if using. Bring to a boil, lower the heat, cover and simmer about 15 minutes.

3. Purée soup in blender or food processor until smooth. Return to pan and reheat. Serve with a swirl of half-and-half in each bowl, if desired.

Makes 4 servings.

Each serving contains:

Cal	Prot	Carb	Fib	Tot. Fat	Sat. Fat	Chol	Sodium
139	5g	21g	8g	4g	1g	0mg	109mg

LETTUCE-AND-GREEN-PEA SOUP WITH MINT

If, like me, you dislike throwing away food this soup provides a good way to use up the tough outside leaves on Cos and Webb lettuces, or indeed any lettuces.

If you do not eat all of the soup at one meal (or if you make a double quantity), you can refrigerate it for two to three days. The flavors will intensify, making an excellent chilled soup.

1/2 cup (125g) fresh mint

3/4 lb. (340g) outer leaves from Cos or romaine lettuce

1 pkg. (10-oz. / 225g) frozen green peas

1 lb. (450g) potatoes, peeled and finely diced

1/2 cup (125ml) dry white wine

1-1/2 cups (375ml) water

1/2 cup (125ml) sour cream

Salt and pepper to taste

1. Strip mint leaves from stalks. Chop half the leaves and set aside.

2. Put lettuce leaves, peas, potatoes, mint stalks and whole mint leaves in a saucepan with wine and water. Bring to a boil and simmer 15 minutes.

3. Purée in a blender or food processor with most of the sour cream, salt and pepper.

4. Pour soup back into pan, add remaining mint and reheat. Serve with a swirl of the remaining sour cream.

Makes 4 servings.

Each serving contains:

Cal	Prot	Carb	Fib	Tot. Fat	Sat. Fat	Chol	Sodium
315	14g	45g	14g	7g	4g	13mg	239mg

BRIE-AND-ONION SOUP

This creamy soup can be made with any soft cheese, such as Brie or Camembert. Though the cheeses used here are French in origin, the soup actually comes from Germany where many creameries now make cheeses similar to their French counterparts.

If you like something that packs a bit more punch, try using a German blue Brie or Cambazola cheese, but remember that heat intensifies the flavor of the cheese.

1 onion, peeled and finely chopped

3 tablespoons (40g) butter

3 tablespoons (25g) flour

1 cup (250ml) vegetable stock, page 10

1 cup (250ml) milk

4 oz. (115g) Brie cheese with the crust removed

Freshly ground black pepper

1. Sauté onion in butter until transparent; do not allow it to brown.
2. Stir in flour then gradually stir in stock and milk. Bring to a boil, stirring constantly.
3. Cut cheese into small pieces and add to soup, stirring until melted. Season with black pepper and cook for 5 minutes.

Makes 4 servings.

Each serving contains:

Cal	Prot	Carb	Fib	Tot. Fat	Sat. Fat	Chol	Sodium
245	9g	13g	1g	18g	11g	56mg	301mg

STRACCIATELLA WITH OYSTER MUSHROOMS

Stracciatella is the classic soup of Latium and the Marches in Central Italy. There it is flavored with nutmeg and lemon zest respectively, both of which are worth trying. I first thought of adding mushrooms after visiting a mushroom farm, and was delighted with the result. Button, shiitake or wild mushrooms will each give you a different flavor.

Note: Semolina is a coarse-ground Durum wheat.

2 eggs

1 tablespoon fine semolina

2 tablespoons finely grated Parmesan cheese, plus extra to serve

1 tablespoon chopped fresh parsley

3-3/4 cups (940ml) vegetable stock, page 10

1 teaspoon brewer's yeast

3 oz. (85g) fresh oyster mushrooms, sliced thinly

1. Beat eggs in a bowl with semolina, Parmesan cheese and parsley. Add 1 cup (250ml) stock and beat until smooth.

2. Mix brewer's yeast with a little stock. Pour into a pan with remaining stock and mushrooms and bring to a boil. Cook for 1 minute.

3. Pour in egg mixture. Beat with a fork for 3-4 minutes until broth returns to a boil and egg cooks into fine shreds. Serve at once with additional cheese.

Makes 4 servings.

Each serving contains:

Cal	Prot	Carb	Fib	Tot. Fat	Sat. Fat	Chol	Sodium
91	6g	10g	2g	3g	1g	96mg	99mg

CURRIED CAULIFLOWER SOUP Ⓥ

Here's a spiced-up version of the French classic cauliflower soup, Crème Dubarry. It is very good served with fried bread croutons. To make them, butter both sides of slices of white bread, sauté over medium heat until crisp, then cut into small cubes.

1 tablespoon cooking oil

1 onion, peeled and coarsely chopped

1/2 teaspoon whole cumin seeds

1/4 cup (60ml) sherry (optional)

1 medium-sized cauliflower, cut into pieces

1/2 teaspoon mild curry powder

3 cups (750ml) vegetable stock, page 10

Salt and pepper to taste

3-4 tablespoons half-and-half (optional)

1. Heat oil in a saucepan and sauté onion and cumin seeds 2-3 minutes to soften the onions. Add sherry, if using, and bring to a boil.

2. Add remaining ingredients except half-and-half, and bring to a boil again. Cover, reduce heat and simmer for 25 minutes.

3. Purée mixture in a blender or food processor, or rub through a sieve. Return to pan and reheat.

4. Swirl half-and-half into each portion, if desired.

Makes 4 servings.

Each serving contains:

Cal	Prot	Carb	Fib	Tot. Fat	Sat. Fat	Chol	Sodium
76	2g	10g	3g	4g	0g	0mg	93mg

CAULIFLOWER CHOWDER

A large helping of this vegetable-packed chowder makes a hearty main course. Serve with crusty whole-wheat rolls and start the meal with Orange-and-Mozzarella Salad (page 41) or Horseradish Carrots with Eggs (page 30). For a change replace half the cauliflower with broccoli.

2 onions, peeled and sliced

1 tablespoon (15g) butter

1 large cauliflower, broken into florets

1 lb. (450g) new potatoes, peeled and quartered or diced

1/4 lb. (115g) frozen peas

1/4 lb. (115g) fresh or frozen corn

3-3/4 cups (940ml) milk

1 bay leaf

Pinch of dried mixed herbs

Salt and pepper to taste

2 tablespoons finely chopped fresh parsley

1. Gently sauté onions in butter until transparent, then add remaining ingredients, reserving a little parsley for garnish.

2. Bring to a boil and cover. Reduce heat to low and simmer gently 15-20 minutes until vegetables are tender. Sprinkle with remaining parsley and serve.

Makes 4 servings.

Each serving contains:

Cal	Prot	Carb	Fib	Tot. Fat	Sat. Fat	Chol	Sodium
309	14g	49g	6g	8g	5g	25mg	265mg

MUSHROOM SOUP

Homemade mushroom soup always seems to have so much more flavor than the canned variety, and it is not difficult to make. Use small button mushrooms for a delicately colored soup, or large field mushrooms for a darker, more robust soup.

1 tablespoon (15g) butter

2 teaspoons cooking oil

1 small onion, peeled and sliced

2 medium leeks, rinsed and sliced

*3/4 lb. (340g) button mushrooms,
wiped and sliced*

1 cup (250ml) milk

*1-1/2 cups (375ml) vegetable
stock, page 10*

1/4 teaspoon dried oregano

1/4 teaspoon celery salt (optional)

Salt and pepper to taste

*3 tablespoons half-and-half or
plain yogurt*

1 tablespoon chopped fresh parsley

1. Heat butter and oil in a large pan and sauté onions and leeks 2-3 minutes. Be careful not to let vegetables brown.

2. Reserve a few slices of mushroom for garnish. Add remaining mushrooms, milk, stock, oregano, celery salt, if using, salt and pepper to the pan. Bring to a boil, cover and simmer for 20 minutes.

3. Purée mixture in a blender or food processor or rub through a sieve. Return to the pan.

4. Stir half-and-half or yogurt into the soup. Bring to a boil, stirring constantly.

5. Serve sprinkled with reserved slices of mushroom and chopped parsley.

Makes 4 servings.

Each serving contains:

Cal	Prot	Carb	Fib	Tot. Fat	Sat. Fat	Chol	Sodium
168	6g	20g	4g	8g	4g	17mg	153mg

MINT-AND-CUCUMBER SOUP

This idea for a cold soup came from my colleague Pete Smith, the cookery editor of *New Woman* magazine. He spikes his version with Pernod but I prefer the cleaner flavor of fresh herbs on their own. Try it both ways and see what you think.

1 large cucumber, roughly chopped
1 clove garlic, peeled and chopped
1/3 cup (25g) fresh mint leaves
2 tablespoons fresh parsley sprigs
3 tablespoons mango chutney
Salt and pepper to taste
3/4 cup (185ml) sour cream

1. Place all ingredients except sour cream in a blender or food processor and blend until smooth.

2. Add sour cream and blend again. Correct the seasoning if necessary.

Makes 4 servings.

Each serving contains:

Cal	Prot	Carb	Fib	Tot. Fat	Sat. Fat	Chol	Sodium
147	4g	13g	3g	9g	6g	19mg	146mg

CHILLED BEET-AND-ORANGE SOUP

Carrots and oranges are often combined in cooking, but I like beets and oranges even better. The idea originated in Eastern Europe where slightly sweet soups are very popular.

Do not use canned pickled beets in this recipe.

1 can (1 lb. / 450g) beets, chopped
Juice of 2 oranges
Grated peel of 1 orange
1 teaspoon ground coriander
1-1/2 cups (375ml) plain yogurt
Salt and pepper to taste

GARNISH
1/4 (60ml) cup plain yogurt
4 sprigs fresh parsley

1. Place soup ingredients in a blender or food processor, reserving a small amount of orange peel for garnish, and mix to a smooth purée.
2. Chill 15-20 minutes before serving.
3. Garnish each serving with a swirl of yogurt, grated orange peel and a sprig of parsley.

Makes 4 servings.

Each serving contains:

Cal	Prot	Carb	Fib	Tot. Fat	Sat. Fat	Chol	Sodium
139	6g	22g	2g	4g	2g	14mg	205mg

MELON-GINGER-AND-AVOCADO SOUP

This unusual cold soup was inspired by the fruit soups of Hungary. It has a lovely flavor and a slightly grainy, but velvety, texture.

1 small melon, halved and seeded

1 large ripe avocado, peeled and pitted

Juice of 1/2 lemon

1/2 cup (125g) low-fat plain yogurt

1/4 cup (60ml) skim milk

1 teaspoon grated fresh ginger

Salt and pepper to taste

1. Reserve 4 thin melon slices for garnish. Peel remaining melon and roughly chop. Place in a blender or food processor with avocado, lemon juice and yogurt.

2. Blend until smooth. Add milk, ginger, salt and pepper and blend again.

3. Chill 15-20 minutes. Garnish with reserved melon slices.

Makes 4 servings.

Each serving contains:

Cal	Prot	Carb	Fib	Tot. Fat	Sat. Fat	Chol	Sodium
165	5g	20g	3g	9g	2g	3mg	124mg

TOMATO-AND-CUCUMBER SOUP

Lots of different versions of this soup have appeared on my table since I first tasted it in Sweden. There, dill is the chosen herb, but tarragon, basil or chives work just as well.

2 cups (500ml) tomato juice

1 large orange

1/2 cup (125g) plain yogurt

2-inch (5cm) piece cucumber, grated

Salt and pepper to taste

Chopped fresh herbs, to taste

1. Pour tomato juice into a bowl; grate in a little orange peel.

2. Squeeze orange and strain juice into the bowl. Whisk in yogurt and stir in cucumber, salt and pepper.

3. Place in refrigerator to chill. Stir in chopped herbs just before serving.

Makes 4 servings.

Each serving contains:

Cal	Prot	Carb	Fib	Tot. Fat	Sat. Fat	Chol	Sodium
64	3g	13g	2g	1g	1g	4mg	522mg

Chapter Two

STARTERS

Whether you need an impressive first course to start a dinner party or a quick dish to keep the family happy while you prepare the rest of the meal, you'll find it in this chapter. I have included both hot and cold starters.

Although these recipes are primarily first courses, they also are good as snacks or side salads. Cheese-and-Walnut Bundles make a delicious snack, for example. Tofu-and-Watercress Pâté can also be used in sandwiches, or to top fingers of toast for canapés at a cocktail party.

For summer gatherings I like to serve Orange-and-Mozzarella Salad. The bright, colorful combination always brings compliments.

ARTICHOKES BAKED WITH GOAT CHEESE

Any kind of fresh, rindless goat cheese can be used in this recipe but I particularly like English Perroche. More economical is the French Roubliac range of goat cheese. These are available in herb- and pepper-coated versions, which add extra flavor to the dish. Remember to leave out the ground pepper if you use pepper-coated cheese.

1 can (15-oz. / 425g) artichoke hearts, drained and cut in halves or quarters

6 oz. (175g) fresh soft goat cheese

6 tablespoons plain yogurt

1 clove of garlic, peeled and crushed

1/4 teaspoon dried thyme

Freshly ground black pepper

6 tablespoons (60g) whole-wheat breadcrumbs

2 tablespoons olive oil

1. Preheat oven to 450F (230C). Arrange artichoke hearts in bottom of an ovenproof dish.

2. Blend goat cheese, yogurt, garlic, thyme and black pepper in a blender or food processor.

3. Spread mixture over artichokes and top with breadcrumbs. Drizzle with olive oil and bake 10-15 minutes until crumbs are brown.

Makes 4 servings.

Each serving contains:

Cal	Prot	Carb	Fib	Tot. Fat	Sat. Fat	Chol	Sodium
273	12g	20g	7g	17g	8g	22mg	318mg

CHEESE-AND-PRUNE PURSES

These parcels make a wonderful starter for a light meal. They may seem a little fussy to make, but I can do it in 10 to 15 minutes while the oven is heating. They then take about 10 minutes to cook—just enough time to prepare a main-course salad.

4 oz. (115g) feta cheese, chopped (1 cup)
1/4 cup (60g) cottage cheese
12 walnut halves
24 large prunes, pitted
12 squares (6-inch / 15cm) filo pastry
Melted butter

1. Heat oven to 400F (200C).
2. Mix cheeses together with a fork and use mixture to sandwich each walnut half between two prunes.
3. Brush pastry squares with melted butter and place a double prune in center of each.
4. Fold edges of pastry over prunes and twist lightly to form purses.
5. Place on an ungreased baking sheet and bake about 10 minutes until crisp and golden.

Makes 4 servings.

Each serving contains:

Cal	Prot	Carb	Fib	Tot. Fat	Sat. Fat	Chol	Sodium
391	10g	42g	5g	22g	12g	57mg	507mg

EGG POTS PROVENÇALE

Serve this dish with melba toast. It goes well with French onion soup and Egyptian Rice, page 152.

1 small onion, peeled and chopped

2 tablespoons olive oil

1 small eggplant, diced

1 zucchini, diced

1 small green bell pepper, seeded and diced

1 small red bell pepper, seeded and diced

4 tomatoes, chopped

1 tablespoon tomato purée

2 tablespoons water

Salt and pepper to taste

4 eggs

1/4 cup (60ml) half-and-half

1 tablespoon freshly grated Parmesan cheese

1. Preheat oven to 400F (200C).

2. Gently sauté onion in oil 2 minutes. Add vegetables and stir-fry 2 minutes longer. Combine tomato purée, water, salt and pepper and pour over vegetables. Cover and cook over low heat 10 minutes.

3. Divide mixture among four ramekin dishes. Make a well in the center of each and break an egg into each one. Top with half-and-half and cheese.

4. Place on a baking sheet and bake 10-12 minutes until egg whites have set but yolks are still soft. Serve at once.

Makes 4 servings.

Each serving contains:

Cal	Prot	Carb	Fib	Tot. Fat	Sat. Fat	Chol	Sodium
215	9g	14g	3g	15g	4g	219mg	194mg

HORSERADISH CARROTS WITH EGGS

This simple mix of ingredients gives a wonderfully delicate balance of flavors. Follow with a thick soup, such as Cauliflower Chowder, page 20, or Broiled Mushrooms with Pesto Sauce, page 107, and rice.

3/4 lb. (340g) carrots, peeled and coarsely grated

1 small onion, peeled and grated

2 tablespoons cooking oil

3 teaspoons creamed horseradish

Salt and pepper to taste

4 eggs

1. Preheat oven to 400F (200C). Generously grease four individual ramekin dishes.

2. Stir-fry vegetables in oil 3-4 minutes until they start to soften. Stir in horseradish, salt and pepper and transfer to the ramekins.

3. Break an egg into each ramekin and bake 15-20 minutes until eggs are set to your liking.

Makes 4 servings.

Each serving contains:

Cal	Prot	Carb	Fib	Tot. Fat	Sat. Fat	Chol	Sodium
179	7g	11g	3g	12g	2g	213mg	164mg

STUFFED RED PEPPERS Ⓥ

I like to make double quantity of these delicately flavored stuffed peppers. One batch is served as soon as it is cooked, while the other is kept in the refrigerator for a day or so to be eaten cold with a good olive-oil-based vinaigrette.

1 small onion, peeled and chopped

1/2 small green bell pepper, seeded and chopped

2 tablespoons olive oil

1/2 teaspoon paprika

1/4 cup (60g) fresh or frozen peas

1 cup (85g) rice

3/4 cup (185ml) vegetable stock, page 10

Salt and pepper to taste

4 small red bell peppers

1. Gently sauté onion and green pepper in 1 tablespoon oil until tender. Stir in paprika, making sure it doesn't burn, and add peas.

2. Stir in rice, remaining oil, stock, salt and pepper. Bring to a boil, stir again, then reduce heat, cover and cook for 15-20 minutes until rice is tender and liquid absorbed.

3. Meanwhile, preheat broiler. Broil red peppers 4-5 minutes, turning once or twice until well-charred.

4. When peppers are cool enough to handle, cut off the tops. Scoop out seeds and fill with cooked rice mixture.

5. Return to broiler for about 5 minutes to warm through.

Makes 4 servings.

Each serving contains:

Cal	Prot	Carb	Fib	Tot. Fat	Sat. Fat	Chol	Sodium
274	5g	45g	4g	8g	1g	0mg	83mg

TOMATOES STUFFED WITH MUSHROOMS Ⓥ

I first tried this recipe with shiitake mushrooms and I was pleased with their delicate flavor. However, ordinary mushrooms can also be used.

8 small tomatoes, with tops cut off

Salt and pepper to taste

1/4 cup (60ml) cooking oil

3/4 lb. (340g) shiitake mushrooms, sliced

2 teaspoons minced fresh tarragon, or 1/2 teaspoon dried tarragon

1 teaspoon chopped fresh thyme, or 1/4 teaspoon dried thyme

Grated lemon peel

1/2 cup (125ml) vegetable stock, page 10, or dry white wine

Fresh parsley sprigs

1. Preheat broiler. Scoop seeds and centers out of tomatoes and discard. Season tomato shells with salt and pepper and place under broiler 2-3 minutes to heat through.

2. Meanwhile, heat oil in a skillet and add remaining ingredients except stock or wine and parsley. Stir-fry over medium heat for 2-3 minutes.

3. Add stock or wine to the pan and boil rapidly over high heat until reduced and thickened.

4. Spoon mushroom mixture into hot tomatoes and serve at once, garnished with parsley.

Makes 4 servings.

Each serving contains:

Cal	Prot	Carb	Fib	Tot. Fat	Sat. Fat	Chol	Sodium
265	5g	30g	6g	15g	2g	0mg	106mg

EGGS WITH SALSA VERDE

In Italy, salsa verde is served with all kinds of cold foods and salads. It is also good poured over warm new potatoes or mixed baby vegetables.

1/2 slice day-old white bread with crust removed, broken into pieces

1 tablespoon white-wine or cider vinegar

5 hard-cooked eggs

2 tablespoons chopped fresh parsley

2 tablespoons chopped fresh basil

1 teaspoon chopped fresh mint

1 teaspoon capers, chopped

3 tablespoons olive oil

Water or lemon juice, if needed

Sprigs of fresh herbs for garnish

1. Soak bread in vinegar for 5 minutes.
2. Meanwhile, peel one egg and rub yolk through a sieve. Chop egg white and use for garnish.
3. Mash soaked bread, then add herbs, capers and sieved egg yolk and mix together.
4. Gradually stir in oil, beating until mixture has a sauce-like consistency. Add water or lemon juice if necessary.
5. Peel remaining eggs and cut in half. Place cut-side down on a large plate or individual plates and top with sauce.

Makes 4 servings.

Each serving contains:

Cal	Prot	Carb	Fib	Tot. Fat	Sat. Fat	Chol	Sodium
199	8g	3g	0g	17g	3g	265mg	125mg

AVOCADO WITH WALNUTS ⓥ

Olive-oil dressings seem to overemphasize the avocado's natural oiliness. Walnut oil, however, has a somewhat bitter note which complements the avocado's creaminess. I added raspberry vinegar for flavor, and chopped walnuts for interest and texture.

1/2 cup (50g) walnut halves
1/2 cup (125ml) walnut oil
1-1/2 tablespoons raspberry
  vinegar
Salt and pepper to taste
2 large ripe avocados
Fresh parsley or chervil sprigs
Fresh raspberries

1. Coarsely chop half the walnuts. Combine with oil, vinegar, salt and pepper.
2. Halve, pit and peel the avocados. Slice each half lengthwise several times then spread out slices in a fan shape.
3. Arrange on four serving plates and dot with remaining walnut halves. Spoon dressing over the top, garnish with parsley or chervil sprigs and raspberries, and serve immediately.

Makes 4 servings.

Each serving contains:

Cal	Prot	Carb	Fib	Tot. Fat	Sat. Fat	Chol	Sodium
492	4g	12g	5g	50g	6g	0mg	79mg

AVOCADO-STUFFED TOMATOES

Avocados are one of my favorite foods so I usually have one or two ripening in my fruit bowl. This mixture of avocado and yogurt is very versatile. As well as using it to fill tomatoes, I stuff stalks of celery or fill small taco shells with it.

4 medium tomatoes
1 large ripe avocado
Juice and grated peel of 1 lemon
2 green onions, finely chopped
1 teaspoon grated fresh ginger
1/2 cup (125g) yogurt
Salt and pepper to taste

1. Cut tomatoes in half. Scoop out seeds and centers and discard. Season lightly and set aside.
2. Peel and pit avocado and immediately coat the flesh with lemon juice to prevent discoloration. Rub avocado through a sieve or process in a blender or food processor. Add remaining lemon juice.
3. Add lemon peel, green onions and ginger. Fold in yogurt, salt and pepper and use to fill prepared tomatoes.

Makes 4 servings.

Each serving contains:

Cal	Prot	Carb	Fib	Tot. Fat	Sat. Fat	Chol	Sodium
130	3g	12g	4g	9g	2g	4mg	98mg

TOFU-AND-WATERCRESS PÂTÉ Ⓥ

This pâté is light and fresh, and very good served with wheat crackers or rye crispbread.

1 bunch watercress, rinsed, trimmed and chopped

6 oz. (175g) tofu, drained

1/4 cup (50g) ground almonds

4 green onions, trimmed and finely chopped

2 tablespoons chopped fresh parsley

1 teaspoon grated lemon peel

Salt and pepper to taste

1. Place all ingredients in a bowl and mix well with a fork.

2. Spoon into a dish or bowl and serve with wheat crackers or rye crispbread.

Makes 4 servings.

Each serving contains:

Cal	Prot	Carb	Fib	Tot. Fat	Sat. Fat	Chol	Sodium
86	6g	4g	2g	6g	1g	0mg	77mg

THREE-FRUIT SALAD Ⓥ

Fruit salad is usually thought of as a dessert, but this mixture makes an excellent first course. Balsamic vinegar is a special vinegar from Modena in Italy. It's made from grape must rather than wine, and is aged for a long time. There are many imitations, so buy the best you can afford. You do not need to use very much at one time, so it will last a long while.

2 kiwi fruit, peeled and sliced
2 persimmons, sliced
2 large tomatoes, sliced
1 cup mixed salad greens
2 tablespoons toasted pine nuts
2 tablespoons black olives
Fresh parsley sprigs

DRESSING
6 tablespoons extra-virgin olive oil
1/4-1/2 teaspoon balsamic vinegar
Salt and pepper to taste

1. Arrange sliced fruits in an overlapping rosette on four individual salad plates.
2. Place greens on the side and dot with pine nuts, black olives and parsley sprigs.
3. Combine dressing ingredients and sprinkle over salad.

Makes 4 servings.

Each serving contains:

Cal	Prot	Carb	Fib	Tot. Fat	Sat. Fat	Chol	Sodium
282	3g	16g	3g	25g	3g	0mg	119mg

RED-PEPPER SALAD Ⓥ

This deceptively simple salad is from the La Mancha region of Central Spain. Broiling the vegetables adds a delicious smoky flavor. If you make it a day or two ahead of time, the flavor will be even better.

4 large red bell peppers, cut in half and seeded

1 large ripe tomato

4 large cloves garlic, with skins on

1/4 cup (60ml) chopped fresh parsley

Salt and pepper to taste

1/4 cup (60ml) extra-virgin olive oil

1 teaspoon wine vinegar

1. Preheat broiler. Broil peppers, tomato and garlic until lightly charred. Let peppers cool slightly. Then, working over a bowl to catch juices, peel them and cut into strips. Peel and chop the tomato.

2. To make dressing: Peel and crush garlic and mix thoroughly with tomato, half the parsley, salt and pepper, using a mortar and pestle or a blender. Add oil, any juice from the peppers, and vinegar.

3. Arrange pepper strips in a serving dish and pour dressing over the top. Sprinkle with remaining chopped parsley. This salad will keep several days in the refrigerator.

4. Serve with a crusty bread.

Makes 4 servings.

Each serving contains:

Cal	Prot	Carb	Fib	Tot. Fat	Sat. Fat	Chol	Sodium
152	1g	8g	2g	14g	2g	0mg	74mg

MUSHROOM-AND-FENNEL SALAD Ⓥ

Mushrooms and fennel are two of my favorite vegetables. Because their flavors blend well together I couldn't resist using them to make this well-textured salad. Serve on a bed of lettuce with crusty brown rolls.

6 oz. (175g) button mushrooms, sliced

3 tablespoons olive or salad oil

1 tablespoon lemon juice

2 fennel bulbs, quartered

1/2 teaspoon ground coriander

2 tablespoons chopped fresh parsley

Salt and pepper to taste

1. Mix mushrooms with oil and lemon juice and set aside.

2. Cook fennel in lightly salted water 5 minutes or until tender-crisp. Drain and plunge into cold water.

3. Drain fennel again and chop finely. Combine with mushrooms, coriander, parsley, salt and pepper.

4. Chill before serving.

Makes 4 servings.

Each serving contains:

Cal	Prot	Carb	Fib	Tot. Fat	Sat. Fat	Chol	Sodium
138	2g	11g	6g	11g	1g	0mg	130mg

ENDIVE-CARROT SALAD WITH MUSHROOMS Ⓥ

I serve this simple gourmet treat at the start of a special meal. Follow it with Glazed-Garlic Tofu, page 86, Braised Spicy Eggplant, page 123, and rice. If endive is not available use mixed salad greens.

4 oz. (115g) oyster mushrooms, cut into large chunks

2 tablespoons light soy sauce

1/2 teaspoon orange peel

1/2 cup (125ml) orange juice

Pinch of Chinese five-spice powder

2 heads of endive, finely sliced

2 carrots, peeled and grated

2 tablespoons salad oil

1 teaspoon sesame oil

Orange segments

Fresh chervil or parsley sprigs

1. Put mushrooms into a saucepan with soy sauce, orange peel and juice and Chinese five-spice powder. Bring to a boil and simmer 1-2 minutes, until mushrooms are cooked. Set aside.

2. Mix endive with carrots and oils.

3. Press endive mixture in ramekin dishes and turn out onto four individual plates.

4. Drain mushrooms and place on top of salads. Garnish with orange segments and chervil or parsley sprigs.

Makes 4 servings.

Each serving contains:

Cal	Prot	Carb	Fib	Tot. Fat	Sat. Fat	Chol	Sodium
175	6g	25g	9g	9g	1g	0mg	503mg

Opposite: Egg Pots Provençale, page 29

ORANGE-AND-MOZZARELLA SALAD

If possible use traditional buffalo-milk mozzarella; it has much more flavor and a better texture than the cow's-milk variety. Avoid Danish block-shaped mozzarella, which is less flavorful. Served with a large piece of Italian bread, this salad also makes a substantial snack.

4 oranges, peeled and sliced
2 balls (7-oz. / 200g) mozzarella cheese, sliced

DRESSING
6 tablespoons extra-virgin olive oil
1 tablespoon wine or cider vinegar
2 tablespoons chopped fresh chervil
Pinch of mixed dried herbs
Salt and pepper to taste

GARNISH
Fresh chervil or parsley sprigs
Pitted black olives, halved or quartered

1. Arrange orange and mozzarella slices in an attractive pattern on four individual plates.
2. Combine dressing ingredients and pour over the salads.
3. Garnish with chervil or parsley sprigs and olives.

Makes 4 servings.

Each serving contains:

Cal	Prot	Carb	Fib	Tot. Fat	Sat. Fat	Chol	Sodium
503	25g	19g	3g	37g	13g	57mg	603mg

Opposite: Orange-and-Mozzarella Salad, above, and Tuscan Soup with Pasta, page 13

AVOCADO SALAD WITH HOT GRAPEFRUIT SAUCE

Grapefruit and avocado is a tried-and-tested combination in my kitchen, but I wanted to use something a little more adventurous than simple grapefruit segments. The result was this deliciously rich sauce which really matches the velvety texture of avocados.

1/4 lb. (115g) mixed greens, such as curly endive, chicory and lettuce

4 large ripe tomatoes, peeled, seeded and finely chopped

3 grapefruit

2 ripe avocados

1 small bunch watercress or garden cress (optional)

6 tablespoons (75g) unsalted butter, cut into small pieces

1. Arrange mixed greens on four individual plates. Place tomatoes in a sieve to drain.

2. Squeeze grapefruit and strain juice into a saucepan. Bring to a boil and boil rapidly until reduced to about 1/4 cup.

3. Meanwhile, halve, peel and pit the avocados. Slice each half lengthwise several times, then spread out to make a fan shape. Arrange on the greens. Top with mounds of tomato and cress, if using.

4. Whisk butter, a piece at a time, into grapefruit juice until mixture thickens. Do not allow it to boil. Pour dressing over salad and serve at once.

Makes 4 servings.

Each serving contains:

Cal	Prot	Carb	Fib	Tot. Fat	Sat. Fat	Chol	Sodium
399	4g	27g	6g	33g	13g	47mg	206mg

CHEESE-AND-WALNUT BUNDLES

I first had this combination in the hill town of San Gimignano in Tuscany, where it was served as a topping for crostini. I still serve it in that way for parties, but I have found that it also makes a very good starter when served in a well-flavored red lettuce.

4 oz. (115g) Pecorino or Edam cheese, diced (1 cup)

1/2 cup (50g) chopped walnuts

1/4 cup (60ml) chopped fresh parsley

1/4 cup (60ml) olive oil

1 tablespoon garlic-flavored wine vinegar

1 clove garlic, crushed

Freshly ground black pepper

4 large lettuce leaves

GARNISH

6-8 cherry tomatoes

Fresh parsley sprigs

1. Place all ingredients, except lettuce leaves and garnishes, in a bowl and mix well together.

2. Spoon mixture onto lettuce leaves and roll into bundles. Garnish with cherry tomatoes and parsley sprigs.

Makes 4 servings.

Each serving contains:

Cal	Prot	Carb	Fib	Tot. Fat	Sat. Fat	Chol	Sodium
340	12g	7g	2g	31g	8g	29mg	350mg

RADICCHIO WITH ORANGE TABBOULEH

This makes a very good starter. It is also popular as finger food to serve with drinks.

1/4 cup (75g) bulgur

1/4 cup (60ml) chopped fresh parsley

Grated peel of 1 orange

1/4 small red bell pepper, seeded and finely chopped

2-1/2 tablespoons olive oil

2 tablespoons lemon juice

1/4 teaspoon ground cinnamon

1/4 teaspoon ground coriander

Salt and pepper to taste

4 radicchio leaves

GARNISH

8 to 12 mandarin orange segments

1. Place bulgur in a bowl and cover with water. Let stand for 20 minutes.

2. Drain well, squeezing out all the water with your fingers. Mix with remaining ingredients except radicchio and orange segments.

3. Arrange radicchio leaves on a large serving plate. Place a spoonful of the bulgur mixture on each leaf. Garnish with mandarin orange segments.

Makes 4 servings.

Each serving contains:

| | | | | Tot. | Sat. | | |
Cal	Prot	Carb	Fib	Fat	Fat	Chol	Sodium
122	2g	11g	2g	9g	1g	0mg	74mg

Chapter Three

SNACKS

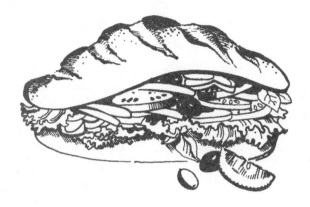

Most of the recipes in this chapter are even faster to prepare than those in the rest of the book. They are designed for the occasions when all you have time for is a quick dash to the pantry or refrigerator and the bare minimum of preparation and cooking. The dishes are both filling and nutritious so do not need any accompaniments.

Bread is the basic ingredient of many of these snacks. It is used for sandwiches or is toasted to make a base for a variety of toppings. These range from the traditional Classic Welsh Rarebit to variations on Italian bruschetta (ciabatta bread topped with olive oil and garlic and sometimes with chopped tomatoes and basil).

Some of the cold snacks, like Pan Bagnat, can be made in advance for lunches or picnics.

The spiced filling for the Mexican Tostados takes about half an hour to make, but if you prepare a large batch when you have time, and store it in the refrigerator or freezer, the dish will be ready in the time it takes to warm the tortillas in the oven.

LIPTAUER CHEESE

This is a wonderfully rich concoction from old-world Hungary. Friends in Budapest press it into a small bowl to turn out and slice. It is delicious eaten in the traditional way, with home-baked rye bread and celery. Or serve with Hungarian Salad, page 75, and lettuce leaves.

6 oz. (175g) cream cheese
1/2 cup (125g) butter, well softened
1 teaspoon paprika
1/2 teaspoon Dijon mustard
1 tablespoon capers, chopped
1 tablespoon chopped fresh chives
Salt and pepper to taste

1. Beat cheese and butter together until well mixed.
2. Beat in remaining ingredients and spoon into a small bowl or large ramekin dish.
3. Chill before serving. If you are in a hurry, pop it in the freezer for 10 minutes, but don't forget it's there!
4. Unmold cheese and cut into wedges to serve.

Makes 4 servings.

Each serving contains:

Cal	Prot	Carb	Fib	Tot. Fat	Sat. Fat	Chol	Sodium
346	3g	2g	0g	37g	24g	105mg	538mg

ANGLO-FRENCH BAGUETTE

Enjoy a French loaf filled with a lively cheese-olive filling.

*1 loaf (8-inch / 20cm) French
bread (baguette)*

*8 oz. (225g) grated sharp Cheddar
cheese (2 cups)*

*1 hard-cooked egg, peeled and
chopped*

4 small gherkins, chopped

4 stuffed olives, chopped

1 teaspoon chopped fresh chives

1/2 teaspoon Dijon mustard

2 tablespoons mayonnaise

Salt and pepper to taste

Lettuce leaves

1. Cut baguette in half length-wise and hollow out a little by removing some of the dough.
2. In a bowl combine remaining ingredients except lettuce. Mix well with a fork.
3. Line bottom half of baguette with lettuce leaves. Cover with cheese mixture. Top with more lettuce and the bread top.
4. Squeeze loaf together with your hands. Slice into 1-inch (2.5cm) lengths to serve.

Makes 4 servings.

Each serving contains:

Cal	Prot	Carb	Fib	Tot. Fat	Sat. Fat	Chol	Sodium
346	17g	11g	1g	26g	13g	117mg	724mg

AVOCADO-TOMATO-AND-FRESH-CILANTRO ROLLS ⓥ

This filling is rather like a chunky version of guacamole. It makes a good snack served on whole-wheat rolls or French bread. I also like it served in warm taco shells or pita bread.

1 ripe avocado, peeled, pitted

2 tomatoes, peeled, seeded and diced

5 small green onions (1 oz. / 25g), trimmed and minced

1 clove garlic, peeled and crushed

1 bunch fresh cilantro or coriander (3 oz. / 85g), chopped

Juice of 1 lemon

Salt and pepper to taste

4 whole-wheat rolls

GARNISH

8 parsley sprigs

1. In a bowl mix together all ingredients, except rolls and parsley.
2. Cut rolls in half and take out a little of the soft center.
3. Mound avocado mixture on each half and garnish with parsley sprigs.

Makes 4 servings.

Each serving contains:

Cal	Prot	Carb	Fib	Tot. Fat	Sat. Fat	Chol	Sodium
99	3g	13g	3g	5g	1g	0mg	126mg

CLASSIC WELSH RAREBIT

This is such a delicious Welsh rarebit that I can eat two helpings at a sitting! However, this quantity will serve four people for a quick snack.

2 tablespoons (25g) butter or margarine

3 tablespoons (25g) flour

1 cup (250ml) beer

1/2 cup (125ml) skim milk

4 oz. (115g) grated Cheddar cheese (1 cup)

1/2 to 1 teaspoon prepared English mustard

Cayenne pepper to taste

4 slices whole-wheat bread, toasted

OPTIONAL FLAVORINGS

1 tablespoon chopped capers

1 tablespoon chopped gherkins

1 tablespoon chopped walnuts

1. Preheat broiler to medium hot. Combine butter or margarine, flour, beer and milk in a saucepan. Stirring constantly, bring to a boil over low heat.

2. When mixture boils and thickens, add cheese and cook 1 minute longer. Stir in mustard, cayenne pepper to taste and any or all of the optional flavorings.

3. Spread the toast generously with cheese mixture. Broil 4-5 minutes until brown.

Makes 4 servings.

Each serving contains:

Cal	Prot	Carb	Fib	Tot. Fat	Sat. Fat	Chol	Sodium
313	13g	26g	3g	17g	10g	46mg	454mg

ORIENTAL CHEESE TOASTS

Very often the simplest foods are the tastiest and this is certainly true of this lightly curried version of cheese on toast. Any kind of chutney can be used, so vary the flavor by experimenting with different types.

4 oz. (115g) grated Cheddar cheese (1 cup)

2 tablespoons ginger chutney

1 teaspoon mild curry powder

4 slices whole-wheat bread

4 tomatoes, sliced

1. Preheat broiler. Mix cheese, chutney and curry powder to a thick paste.

2. Toast the bread, then top each slice with tomatoes. Spread cheese mixture over the top and broil 3-4 minutes until cheese is bubbly.

Makes 4 servings.

Each serving contains:

Cal	Prot	Carb	Fib	Tot. Fat	Sat. Fat	Chol	Sodium
241	12g	26g	4g	11g	6g	30mg	391mg

CHEESE-AND-SALSA TOASTS

I love cheese on toast in any shape or form. This version uses a Mexican-style salsa to give a spicy finish, making a change from the usual Worcestershire sauce. If you have time, make a double quantity of the salsa and refrigerate to use with tacos or grilled vegetables.

4 thick slices country bread, or 1 Italian or French loaf (8-9-inch / 20-22.5cm) cut open lengthwise

1/4 cup (60ml) extra-virgin olive oil

6 oz. (175g) grated aged Cheddar cheese (1-1/2 cups)

SALSA

2 tomatoes, peeled and minced

1 green chile pepper, seeded and chopped

4 green onions, trimmed and minced

1/2 small pickle, minced

3 tablespoons chopped fresh parsley, basil or cilantro

1 clove garlic, peeled and minced (optional)

1. Preheat broiler. Combine all salsa ingredients. Set aside.

2. Brush both sides of bread slices with olive oil and toast on each side.

3. Spread cheese evenly over toast. Spoon salsa down the middle.

4. Return to broiler and serve as soon as cheese starts to bubble.

Makes 4 servings.

Each serving contains:

Cal	Prot	Carb	Fib	Tot. Fat	Sat. Fat	Chol	Sodium
339	12g	10g	2g	28g	11g	45mg	431mg

EGG-AND-ZUCCHINI BAKE

This all-in-one dish is really easy to prepare. Add buttered potatoes or crusty rolls to turn it into a complete meal. A tomato salad dressed with a yogurt-and-fresh-herb dressing makes a good starter.

1/2 lb. (225g) zucchini, diced

2 tablespoons (25g) butter

1 clove garlic, peeled and crushed

6 green onions, trimmed and chopped

1 can (14-oz. / 400g) lima beans

5 eggs

1/4 cup (60ml) milk

3 oz. (75g) grated Cheddar cheese (3/4 cup)

Salt and pepper to taste

1. Preheat oven to 350F (180C).

2. Gently sauté zucchini in butter 2-3 minutes until it begins to soften. Add garlic and green onions and cook two minutes longer. Stir in lima beans and transfer to an ovenproof dish.

3. Beat eggs and milk together and stir in cheese, salt and pepper. Pour mixture over vegetables. Bake about 20 minutes until puffed and golden.

Makes 4 servings.

Each serving contains:

Cal	Prot	Carb	Fib	Tot. Fat	Sat. Fat	Chol	Sodium
311	19g	18g	4g	20g	10g	305mg	703mg

MUSHROOM BRUSCHETTA ⓥ

With the popularity of Mediterranean-style food, chefs and cooks have felt free to add all kinds of different toppings to Italian bread to make creative variations of bruschetta. Here is one of my favorites.

2 cloves garlic, peeled and crushed

6 tablespoons extra-virgin olive oil

8 large fresh mushrooms

Salt and pepper to taste

1/4 cup (60ml) white wine

1 Italian ciabatta loaf, halved lengthwise, and crosswise

2 tomatoes, peeled, seeded and chopped

2 tablespoons chopped fresh parsley

2 tablespoons chopped fresh green onion

1. Preheat broiler. Mix garlic and olive oil and use 3-4 tablespoons to brush the underside of the mushrooms. Sprinkle mushrooms with salt and place on a broiler pan. Sprinkle with white wine and broil 4-5 minutes until cooked through.

2. Meanwhile, brush remaining garlic oil over the bread.

3. Toast the bread. Arrange mushrooms on toasted bread.

4. Mix tomatoes, parsley, onion, more salt and pepper. Sprinkle over mushrooms. Place under the broiler for 1-2 minutes. Serve at once.

Makes 4 servings.

Each serving contains:

Cal	Prot	Carb	Fib	Tot. Fat	Sat. Fat	Chol	Sodium
235	2g	9g	2g	21g	3g	0mg	120mg

EGGPLANT-AND-MOZZARELLA BRUSCHETTA

This is another of the many variations of simple Italian bruschetta I dream up almost every week. Each one is a little different, but extra-virgin olive oil and garlic remain constant.

1 lb. (450g) eggplant, trimmed

1 Italian ciabatta loaf, halved lengthwise, then crosswise

1 clove garlic, halved

2 tablespoons extra-virgin olive oil

2 tablespoons tomato purée

12 fresh basil leaves

1 ball (7-oz. / 200g) mozzarella cheese, sliced

Salt and pepper to taste

1. Preheat broiler. Slice eggplant and broil on both sides until cooked through and golden. Cut off skin, if desired.

2. Toast cut sides of bread under the broiler.

3. Rub toasted surfaces with garlic, then brush with olive oil. Spread each surface thinly with tomato purée. Return to broiler until toasted.

4. Cover bread with eggplant slices and top with basil leaves, mozzarella, salt and pepper. Return to broiler until cheese melts. Drizzle with remaining olive oil just before serving.

Makes 4 servings.

Each serving contains:

Cal	Prot	Carb	Fib	Tot. Fat	Sat. Fat	Chol	Sodium
254	11g	13g	3g	18g	8g	39mg	330mg

ITALIAN SAGE TOAST

I have added fresh sage leaves to my version of that wonderful Italian invention—Mozzarella in Carozza, or fried mozzarella-cheese sandwich. The result is a mouthwatering snack that disappears in seconds!

2 eggs

Salt and pepper to taste

4 thick slices whole-wheat bread

3 tablespoons chopped fresh sage

2 balls (7-oz. / 200g) mozzarella cheese, sliced

1. Beat eggs, salt and pepper and pour into a shallow dish.

2. Dip bread slices in egg mixture so they are well coated and all the egg is absorbed.

3. Preheat broiler. In a non-stick skillet cook the bread until golden on both sides. Remove from pan and place on broiler pan. Sprinkle with sage.

4. Arrange cheese on sage-topped fried bread. Broil until bubbly. Serve at once.

Makes 4 servings.

Each serving contains:

Cal	Prot	Carb	Fib	Tot. Fat	Sat. Fat	Chol	Sodium
402	26g	19g	2g	25g	14g	184mg	653mg

MEXICAN TOSTADOS WITH SPICED LENTILS Ⓥ

The aroma of tortillas heating in the oven conjures up visions of ponchos, sombreros and passionate guitar music!

1 large onion, peeled and finely
chopped

2 cloves garlic, peeled and crushed

1 teaspoon dried thyme

1 teaspoon ground cumin

1 teaspoon ground coriander

2 tablespoons cooking oil

Salt and pepper to taste

8 oz. (225g) red or yellow
split lentils

2 tablespoons tomato purée

2 teaspoons brewer's yeast

2 cups (500ml) water

2 large red bell peppers

2 green chile peppers

8 tortillas

1. Sauté onion, garlic, thyme and spices in oil 3-4 minutes to soften the vegetables. Add remaining ingredients except peppers and tortillas. Stir and bring to a boil.

2. Reduce heat and simmer 20-25 minutes until lentils are softened but not mushy.

3. Meanwhile, preheat broiler. Seed the bell peppers and cut into quarters. Cut chiles in half and remove the seeds.

4. Broil peppers until charred; remove skins.

5. Heat tortillas as directed on package.

6. Spread 4 tortillas with some of the cooked lentils. Place peppers on top and add remaining lentils. Top with remaining tortillas.

Makes 4 servings.

Each serving contains:

Cal	Prot	Carb	Fib	Tot. Fat	Sat. Fat	Chol	Sodium
400	13g	61g	7g	12g	2g	0mg	444mg

FALAFEL IN PITA BREAD ⓥ

Chickpeas, also known as *garbanzos,* work well in this quick version of Egyptian falafel.

1 can (8 oz. / 225g) chickpeas or garbanzos, drained

1 onion, peeled and minced

2 cloves garlic, peeled and minced

1 teaspoon baking powder

1 teaspoon cumin seed

1 teaspoon coriander

2 tablespoons parsley

Salt and pepper to taste

1 tablespoon lemon juice

1 tablespoon all-purpose flour

1 tablespoon fine oatmeal

Vegetable oil for deep frying

4 small pita breads

Shredded lettuce and watercress

1. Rub chickpeas or garbanzos through a sieve, or process in a food processor. Add onion, garlic, baking powder, spices, parsley, salt, pepper and lemon juice; mix to a smooth paste. Roll into walnut-sized balls.

2. Mix flour and oatmeal together; roll chickpea balls in mixture until well coated.

3. Heat oil in a deep fryer to 350F (180C). Fry the chickpea balls (falafel) in batches 5-6 minutes, until golden in color.

4. Meanwhile, preheat broiler. Toast pita bread on both sides, cut in half and slit open.

5. Fill pita bread with lettuce, watercress and falafel.

Makes 4 servings.

Each serving contains:

Cal	Prot	Carb	Fib	Tot. Fat	Sat. Fat	Chol	Sodium
316	12g	55g	5g	6g	1g	0mg	522mg

PAN BAGNAT

In the summer these deliciously filling rolls are sold all along the Mediterranean coast at beach cafés and stalls. They are usually filled with tuna or anchovy as well as eggs, olives, onions and tomatoes, but they lose nothing by omitting the fish. Traditionally, pan bagnat is wrapped firmly and weighted for an hour or so, allowing flavors to mingle and bread to moisten.

4 large flat rolls or hamburger buns

1/4 cup (60ml) extra-virgin olive oil

10-12 lettuce leaves

2 large beef-steak tomatoes, thinly sliced

6 hard-cooked eggs, peeled and sliced

1 small onion, peeled and sliced into thin rings

16-20 black olives, pitted and halved

8 large sprigs basil or parsley

1. Cut each roll into two flat halves and brush cut surfaces with olive oil.

2. Place lettuce and tomatoes on bottom half of each roll. Top with eggs, onion rings, olives and basil or parsley.

3. Cover with tops of rolls and serve.

Makes 4 servings.

Each serving contains:

Cal	Prot	Carb	Fib	Tot. Fat	Sat. Fat	Chol	Sodium
393	14g	28g	4g	25g	5g	319mg	534mg

CORN-AND-POTATO FRITTERS

This simple variation on the popular Jewish potato cakes, *latkes*, is very quick to make. It is delicious served with yellow-tomato salsa, page 108.

2 lb. (900g) potatoes, coarsely
    grated

6 oz. (175g) drained canned,
    or frozen, corn kernels

2 eggs, beaten

Salt and pepper to taste

1-2 tablespoons cooking oil
    for frying

Salsa

1. Drain any liquid from potatoes, then mix with corn, eggs, salt and pepper.

2. Heat oil in a heavy-based skillet and drop in spoonfuls of potato mixture.

3. Cook in batches over medium heat 4-5 minutes on each side until crisp and golden. Check that potato is cooked through before serving with your favorite salsa.

Makes 4 servings.

Each serving contains:

				Tot.	Sat.		
Cal	Prot	Carb	Fib	Fat	Fat	Chol	Sodium
332	9g	56g	4g	10g	2g	106mg	229mg

FENNEL-AND-POTATO ROSTI

I became addicted to Swiss rosti on my first visit to Switzerland; the simple potato mixture has provided an excellent base for endless variations. This one includes one of my favorite vegetables—fennel.

Buy the smallest fennel bulbs you can find. They are less stringy and, with less to discard, they're more economical than large ones.

3-4 small fennel bulbs

2 lb. (900g) potatoes, peeled and cut into chunks

Salt and pepper to taste

1 tablespoon butter

1 onion, peeled and finely chopped

1 clove garlic, finely chopped

1 teaspoon fennel seeds

1. Trim fronds from fennel, and set aside. Trim base and stems and cut in half.

2. Place fennel halves in a pan with potatoes and cover with water. Bring to a boil, add salt and simmer 15 minutes until almost tender. Drain and slice fennel and potato chunks.

3. Heat butter in a heavy-based non-stick skillet and sauté fennel fronds, onion, garlic and fennel seeds 2-3 minutes.

4. Add fennel and potato and press down with spatula. Sprinkle with salt and pepper. Cook over medium heat 6-8 minutes until bottom is brown. Turn over and cook 6 minutes until the other side is browned.

Makes 4 servings.

Each serving contains:

Cal	Prot	Carb	Fib	Tot. Fat	Sat. Fat	Chol	Sodium
306	7g	65g	13g	4g	2g	8mg	230mg

CHEESE-AND-BEAN ROSTI

This quick recipe for rosti differs from real Swiss rosti in that it is made with raw potatoes which have been grated instead of with potatoes which have been boiled in their skins and cooled. If you use leftover potatoes, you will not need the egg.

1/4 cup (50g) butter

1 lb. (450g) potatoes, peeled and grated

1 can (7 oz. / 200g) kidney or pinto beans, drained

1 egg, beaten

3 oz. (85g) shredded Cheddar cheese (3/4 cup)

1 oz. (25g) freshly grated Parmesan cheese (2 tablespoons)

1 tablespoon chopped fresh chives

1 tablespoon chopped fresh parsley

Salt and pepper to taste

1. Heat half the butter in a non-stick skillet.

2. Mix potatoes with remaining ingredients and spoon into skillet. Press down to distribute evenly. Cook over medium heat about 10 minutes.

3. Slide rosti onto a large plate. Melt remaining butter in skillet and invert rosti into pan with cooked side up. Cook another 10 minutes until cooked through.

Makes 4 servings.

Each serving contains:

Cal	Prot	Carb	Fib	Tot. Fat	Sat. Fat	Chol	Sodium
399	16g	35g	5g	22g	13g	112mg	470mg

ROSTI WITH POACHED EGGS

Here is another quick variation on the Swiss specialty, teamed with poached eggs. Tomato and parsley add a colorful touch.

1-1/2 lb. (675g) potatoes, grated
1 small onion, peeled and grated
1 tablespoon flour
5 eggs
Salt and pepper to taste
Cooking oil

GARNISH
4 slices tomato
Fresh parsley sprig

1. Squeeze grated vegetables dry and mix together.
2. Beat flour with 1 egg and pour over vegetables. Season with salt and pepper and mix again.
3. Heat a little oil in a heavy-based skillet and spread potato mixture evenly in pan. Cook over medium heat 8-10 minutes.
4. Turn over with a large spatula, and cook another 8-10 minutes.
5. Meanwhile, break remaining eggs into buttered egg poachers and season with salt and pepper. Cover and poach 5-6 minutes until cooked to your liking. Serve eggs on top of rosti. Garnish with tomato slices and parsley.

Makes 4 servings.

Each serving contains:

Cal	Prot	Carb	Fib	Tot. Fat	Sat. Fat	Chol	Sodium
316	11g	39g	3g	13g	3g	266mg	156mg

LA MANCHA-STYLE VEGETABLES WITH EGGS

The vegetable base of this authentic Spanish recipe has certain similarities to the better-known French *ratatouille* and *piperade*. Eggs are lightly stirred in, making it a more substantial snack. Serve with crusty bread or toasted croutons.

1/2 onion, peeled and chopped

1 clove garlic, peeled and crushed

3 tablespoons olive oil

2 green peppers, seeded and chopped

1 red pepper, seeded and chopped

1 lb. (450g) tomatoes

1 lb. (450g) zucchini, trimmed and chopped

Salt to taste

1/2 teaspoon sugar (optional)

2 eggs, beaten

1. In large skillet sauté onion and garlic in olive oil until golden. Add peppers, cover and continue cooking.

2. Meanwhile, pour boiling water over tomatoes and let stand for a few minutes. Peel and remove seeds. Add to pan, crushing down vegetables with a wooden spoon. Cook, uncovered, over low heat about 5 minutes.

3. Before tomato liquid has completely evaporated, add zucchini to pan. When zucchini begin to change color, add salt. Add sugar if desired.

4. Cook over low heat until vegetables are tender. Add eggs, stir once or twice, then cook until set. Serve with crusty bread or toasted croutons.

Makes 4 servings.

Each serving contains:

Cal	Prot	Carb	Fib	Tot. Fat	Sat. Fat	Chol	Sodium
196	8g	14g	4g	14g	2g	106mg	113mg

Chapter Four

SALADS

Many of the recipes in this chapter can be served as side salads with cooked dishes or as part of a medley of salads. For example, Red-Cabbage-and-Sour-Cream Salad, Apple-Date-and-Endive Salad and Watercress-and-Pistachio Salad make a very good combination. Other recipes, such as Mustard-and-Brie Leafy Salad, Stuffed-Pepper Salad and Orange-and-Goat-Cheese Salad are substantial enough for a main course.

Many of my side salads are easily made in a matter of minutes, using whatever I happen to have on hand. I add an interesting dressing, such as the yogurt-based one in Grape Salad, the dressing flavored with balsamic vinegar that I added to the Three-Fruit Salad, or the mustard-based dressing used in the Mustard-and-Brie Leafy Salad.

A sprinkling of toasted nuts or sunflower seeds adds a nice texture to any mixed green salad. Crumbled herb-flavored feta cheese quickly turns the ordinary into the extraordinary.

WARM CARROT SALAD WITH ARUGULA Ⓥ

The Moors occupied the southern half of Spain for 700 years, so it's not surprising that their influence lingers on in the exotic flavors of some of the dishes, such as this carrot salad from Granada. Arugula is a peppery-flavored green also known as *rocket*.

1/2 lb. (225g) carrots, sliced

1/4 cup (60ml) extra-virgin olive oil

Freshly ground black pepper

1 teaspoon ground cumin

1/4 cup (75g) red kidney beans

Juice of 1/2 lemon

2 tablespoons sherry vinegar

1 teaspoon honey

Arugula or Romaine leaves

1. Place the carrots in a saucepan with 1 tablespoon oil, pepper and cumin. Barely cover with water and bring to a boil.

2. Cook over medium heat 7 minutes until liquid has boiled away and carrots are tender. Do not let carrots burn. Remove from heat.

3. Add kidney beans and toss together. Mix remaining oil with lemon juice, vinegar and honey and add to vegetables.

4. Arrange arugula or Romaine on individual serving plates and top with vegetables and dressing.

Makes 4 servings.

Each serving contains:

Cal	Prot	Carb	Fib	Tot. Fat	Sat. Fat	Chol	Sodium
167	2g	11g	2g	14g	2g	0mg	55mg

RED-CABBAGE-AND-SOUR-CREAM SALAD

This makes a colorful salad. If red cabbages are not available firm green cabbage can be used instead. Grate the cabbage with a coarse grater as this gives a much better texture than trying to shred it—even with a sharp knife I never seem to be able to get it fine enough.

1/2 red cabbage
3 stalks celery
9 green onions
1/2 cup (50g) walnut halves
3 tablespoons sour cream
Salt and pepper to taste

1. Coarsely grate the cabbage and finely chop the celery and green onions. Coarsely chop the walnuts.

2. Place all ingredients in a large bowl and toss together. Serve at once.

Makes 4 servings.

Each serving contains:

Cal	Prot	Carb	Fib	Tot. Fat	Sat. Fat	Chol	Sodium
145	4g	9g	3g	12g	2g	5mg	109mg

GRAPE SALAD Ⓥ

If you live near a Greek grocery store or a good delicatessen, you will be able to buy grape leaves packed in brine. These make a very attractive lining for the salad bowl, but warn everyone not to eat them—they are very tough!

1/2 lb. (225g) seedless white grapes, halved

1 small cucumber, diced

3 stalks celery, minced

1 small green bell pepper, seeded and minced

1 tablespoon raisins or sultanas

Grape or Romaine leaves, if desired

DRESSING

2 tablespoons plain yogurt

1 teaspoon lemon juice

1/4 teaspoon dried rosemary

1. Place salad ingredients in a bowl and toss well together.
2. Spoon into a serving dish lined, if desired, with whole grape or Romaine leaves.
3. Beat dressing ingredients together until blended. Pour over the salad, toss and serve.

Makes 4 servings.

Each serving contains:

Cal	Prot	Carb	Fib	Tot. Fat	Sat. Fat	Chol	Sodium
67	1g	16g	1g	1g	0g	1mg	32mg

APPLE-DATE-AND-ENDIVE SALAD Ⓥ

This is a very refreshing salad to serve with Corn-and-Potato Fritters, page 59, or Grilled Feta Cheese with Olives, page 109.

2 apples
Juice of 1/4 lemon
4 large heads endive, sliced
8-10 pitted and chopped dates
1 tablespoon olive oil
Pinch of dried mixed herbs
Ground black pepper to taste

GARNISH
Chopped fresh parsley

1. Core the apples and cut into small pieces. Immediately toss in lemon juice.
2. Add remaining ingredients and toss together thoroughly.
3. Serve at once with a sprinkling of chopped fresh parsley.

Makes 4 servings.

Each serving contains:

Cal	Prot	Carb	Fib	Tot. Fat	Sat. Fat	Chol	Sodium
137	1g	28g	4g	4g	1g	0mg	12mg

ZUCCHINI SALAD Ⓥ

This makes a delicious starter or it can be served as a side salad or as part of a buffet. To make a more-substantial dish add 4 chopped hard-cooked eggs or 1/2 cup diced aged Cheddar or Gouda cheese. If you do this it will, of course, no longer be suitable for vegans.

1 lb. (450g) zucchini, trimmed and diced

4 tomatoes, peeled and diced

3 green onions, trimmed and diced

1 tablespoon chopped fresh cilantro or coriander

1 green chile pepper, halved, seeded and chopped

2 tablespoons olive oil

1 teaspoon wine vinegar or cider vinegar

Salt and pepper to taste

1. Steam zucchini 3-4 minutes, drain and let cool.

2. Toss all ingredients together. Serve at once

Makes 4 servings.

Each serving contains:

Cal	Prot	Carb	Fib	Tot. Fat	Sat. Fat	Chol	Sodium
109	3g	11g	3g	7g	1g	0mg	83mg

ITALIAN BEAN SALAD Ⓥ

Look for Italian borlotti beans or pinto beans for this salad from southern Italy. The beans have pretty pink strands running through the skins which look very attractive in the salad. If you cannot find them, cannellini beans taste almost as good.

1 large red bell pepper, cut into quarters

1 tablespoon capers

20 black olives, pitted and chopped

1 tablespoon chopped fresh parsley

1 can (14-oz. / 400g) borlotti, pinto or cannellini beans, drained

DRESSING

1/4 cup (60ml) extra-virgin olive oil

1 tablespoon wine or cider vinegar

1 teaspoon Dijon mustard

Salt and pepper to taste

1. Place bell pepper quarters, skin-side up, under a hot broiler until well charred. Remove from heat and set aside. When cool peel off charred skin and dice the flesh.

2. Mix peppers with remaining ingredients in a large bowl.

3. Mix dressing ingredients together, pour over salad and toss to coat. Serve at once.

Makes 4 servings.

Each serving contains:

Cal	Prot	Carb	Fib	Tot. Fat	Sat. Fat	Chol	Sodium
230	4g	17g	5g	16g	2g	0mg	580mg

WATERCRESS-AND-PISTACHIO SALAD ⓥ

This is very much a pantry salad. You can add ingredients according to what you have on hand—baby artichoke hearts, onions in oil, olives, canned pimento strips, or toast rounds spread with olive paste, for example.

Sun-dried tomatoes packed in oil are quicker to use than those sold dried because the latter must be soaked in boiling water for 15 minutes before draining and cutting into thin strips.

1 bunch of watercress or watercress tossed with lamb's lettuce or baby leaves

3 tablespoons toasted pistachios

1 tablespoon toasted pine nuts

3-4 pieces sun-dried tomatoes, cut into thin strips

Fresh basil or parsley sprigs

DRESSING

1/4 cup (60ml) extra-virgin olive oil

1 tablespoon well-flavored vinegar such as sherry, tarragon or orange

Salt and pepper to taste

1. Place lettuce leaves on 4 salad plates. Sprinkle with nuts and tomato strips. Dot with chosen additions and sprigs of herbs.

2. Beat dressing ingredients together and spoon on at the last minute. Serve at once.

Makes 4 servings.

Each serving contains:

				Tot.	Sat.		
Cal	Prot	Carb	Fib	Fat	Fat	Chol	Sodium
181	1g	4g	1g	19g	3g	0mg	111mg

GREEN MANGO SALAD

Very often mangoes arrive in the stores when they are still green. Rather than wait for them to ripen, try this deliciously tangy salad. Serve with Curried Beans, page 100, and one of the rice dishes in Chapter 9.

2 tablespoons plain yogurt

Pinch of salt

1/2 teaspoon vegetarian Worcestershire sauce (Angostura®)

1 teaspoon vinegar

Juice of 1/2 lime

1 green mango, peeled and grated

1. Mix yogurt, salt, Worcester-shire sauce, vinegar and lime juice together.

2. Add mango and toss well.

Makes 4 servings.

Each serving contains:

Cal	Prot	Carb	Fib	Tot. Fat	Sat. Fat	Chol	Sodium
41	1g	10g	1g	0g	0g	1mg	78mg

Opposite: Cheese-and-Prune Purses, page 28

ORANGE-AND-DATE SALAD Ⓥ

This fresh-tasting salad comes from Morocco, where it is often served before a filling dish like couscous. It also makes an excellent side salad with Bulgur-and-Nut Pilaf, page 160.

Fresh dates are used in the original recipe. Dried dates can be used, but you will not need to use quite as many.

For an interesting variation, replace dates with a similar amount of chopped black olives.

3 large thin-skinned oranges, peeled and pith removed

Juice of 1 lemon

2 teaspoons sugar

Pinch of salt

6-8 Cos or Romaine lettuce leaves

8-10 fresh dates, chopped

1/3 cup (30g) blanched almonds

Ground cinnamon

1. Cut out orange segments from between the membranes, reserving juice.

2. Mix reserved orange juice with lemon juice, sugar and salt.

3. Tear lettuce leaves into pieces and carefully toss with orange segments. Spoon into a bowl and pour dressing over.

4. Scatter dates and almonds over salad, then top with a dash of cinnamon. Serve at once.

Makes 4 servings.

Each serving contains:

Cal	Prot	Carb	Fib	Tot. Fat	Sat. Fat	Chol	Sodium
191	4g	38g	6g	5g	0g	0mg	71mg

Opposite: Italian Bean Salad, page 70

FENNEL-AND-ENDIVE SALAD Ⓥ

This salad works well as part of a salad buffet but it is also very good served with Empedrado Madrileño, page 156, or Balaton Hotpot, page 94. You may also add cubes of cheese or chopped hard-cooked eggs to turn it into a main-course salad (not for vegans) and serve with crusty bread or a rice salad.

2 small fennel bulbs
2 apples
1 tablespoon lemon juice
2 heads of endive
2 tablespoons extra-virgin olive oil
Salt and pepper to taste

1. Trim fennel, reserving any green fronds for garnish. Cut fennel bulbs into quarters.

2. Plunge fennel quarters into boiling water and blanch 1 minute. Drain and plunge into cold water. Set aside.

3. Core apples and cut into small dice. Toss in lemon juice to stop them from discoloring.

4. Cut endive into thick strips and mix with apples.

5. Drain fennel and cut into thin sticks; add to endive and apples. Add oil, salt and pepper. Toss and serve garnished with fennel fronds.

Makes 4 servings.

Each serving contains:

Cal	Prot	Carb	Fib	Tot. Fat	Sat. Fat	Chol	Sodium
141	2g	20g	6g	7g	1g	0mg	133mg

HUNGARIAN SALAD Ⓥ

Many of the salads I've had in Hungary are marinated overnight in a light sweet-and-sour dressing, which gives them a nice flavor. However, if you haven't time to wait you can achieve a similar flavor by mixing sweet-and-sour cucumbers, which are available in jars or loose in delicatessens, into a fresh vegetable salad.

1/2 cup sliced sweet pickles

1 small cucumber, very thinly sliced

1 small red bell pepper, seeded

1 carrot, peeled, coarsely grated

2 tablespoons lemon juice

Pinch of paprika

Pinch of caraway seeds

1. Put pickles and cucumber in a bowl with 2 tablespoons liquid from the pickle jar.
2. Shred red bell pepper thinly. Add pepper and carrot to pickle-cucumber mixture.
3. Add lemon juice, paprika and caraway and toss. Chill until serving.

Makes 4 servings.

Each serving contains:

Cal	Prot	Carb	Fib	Tot. Fat	Sat. Fat	Chol	Sodium
30	1g	7g	1g	0g	0g	0mg	90mg

MUSTARD-AND-BRIE LEAFY SALAD

Serve this attractive salad as a main course for summer suppers or cut the quantities and serve as a first course. Follow it with Braised Spicy Eggplant, page 123, and Singapore Noodles, page 147.

2 oz. (50g) lamb's lettuce

1/2 head red-leaf lettuce

1/2 small head Boston or butter lettuce

1/2 small cucumber, finely sliced

3/4 lb. (225g) Brie cheese, sliced

12 kumquats, sliced

Fresh chervil sprigs

DRESSING

1/2 cup (125ml) olive oil

2 tablespoons lemon juice

3 tablespoons English whole-grain mustard

Salt and pepper to taste

1. Arrange lettuces on four individual plates, keeping each one separate from the others and taking up about three-quarters of the plate. Fill in the gap with sliced cucumber.

2. Arrange cheese slices just off the center of the plate. Dot with kumquats and chervil.

3. Mix dressing ingredients together and pour over the salad. Serve at once.

Makes 4 servings.

Each serving contains:

Cal	Prot	Carb	Fib	Tot. Fat	Sat. Fat	Chol	Sodium
595	21g	16g	6g	52g	19g	85mg	776mg

ORANGE-AND-GOAT-CHEESE SALAD

This salad can be made with different kinds of goat cheese to suit your personal preference. Choose from Roubliac fresh goat cheese coated in herbs or paprika or an aged St. Maure.

Lettuce leaves

1/2 bunch watercress, trimmed

12 oz. (340g) small log-shaped goat cheeses, sliced

2 oranges, peeled, trimmed and segmented

12 walnut halves, coarsely chopped

DRESSING

6 tablespoons olive oil

1 tablespoon orange juice

1 tablespoon vinegar

Grated orange rind

Salt and pepper to taste

1. Tear lettuce leaves into small pieces and mix with watercress. Place on four individual salad plates.

2. Arrange four to five slices of goat cheese in the center of each plate. Place orange segments around cheese and sprinkle with walnuts.

3. Beat dressing ingredients together until blended. Pour over salad and serve at once.

Makes 4 servings.

Each serving contains:

Cal	Prot	Carb	Fib	Tot. Fat	Sat. Fat	Chol	Sodium
563	20g	12g	2g	49g	21g	67mg	507mg

STUFFED-PEPPER SALAD

Serve these attractive pepper rings with a salad and crusty whole-wheat rolls. If you do not eat both bell peppers, the remaining one can be stored, uncut, in the refrigerator for two to three days.

2 red, green or yellow bell peppers

8-10 oz. (225-280g) cream cheese

1/2 cup (50g) mixed peanuts and raisins, finely chopped

6 green onions, trimmed, finely chopped

2 small stalks celery, finely chopped

1 teaspoon grated fresh ginger (optional)

Salt and pepper to taste

TO SERVE

Mixed salad greens

Cherry tomatoes

Sprigs of fresh herbs

1. Cut tops off bell peppers and scoop out seeds. Trim off any flesh from the cut tops and chop finely.

2. Place cheese in a bowl and add chopped pepper, nuts and raisins, green onions, celery and ginger, if using. Mix well together and season to taste.

3. Spoon cheese mixture into scooped-out peppers and press down. Cover with plastic wrap and chill.

4. Just before serving, cut stuffed peppers into slices, using a sharp knife. Arrange mixed salad greens on serving plates and place pepper slices on top. Dot with cherry tomatoes and sprigs of herbs.

Makes 4 servings.

Each serving contains:

Cal	Prot	Carb	Fib	Tot. Fat	Sat. Fat	Chol	Sodium
347	8g	15g	3g	29g	17g	78mg	300mg

ZUCCHINI-AND-DILL MOLDED SALADS Ⓥ

Molded salads like this look very attractive on the plate. They make a good centerpiece for a cold meal or they can be served as a first course. Follow with Sicilian Potatoes, page 89, and Chickpeas with Spinach, page 93. Or serve as a simple main course with jacket potatoes.

1/2 lb. (225g) zucchini, trimmed and coarsely grated

2 small carrots, peeled, grated

1/4 small green bell pepper, seeded and finely shredded

1/4 cup (50g) cottage cheese or tofu

2 tablespoons chopped fresh dill

Salt and pepper to taste

Mixed salad greens

1. Mix zucchini, carrots and green bell pepper together.
2. Add cottage cheese or tofu, dill, salt and pepper and mix well.
3. Spoon mixture into four small ramekin dishes, pressing down well.
4. Turn out on a bed of small mixed salad greens and serve at once.

Makes 4 servings.

Each serving contains:

Cal	Prot	Carb	Fib	Tot. Fat	Sat. Fat	Chol	Sodium
35	2g	6g	2g	1g	0g	0mg	82mg

ORIENTAL SALAD PLATTER

It's easy to vary this dish according to the vegetables you have on hand. Rutabaga or turnip can be used in place of celery root. Another unusual mixture with a good flavor and color is beets with celery root. Shredded Chinese leaves or watercress can replace the bean sprouts.

1/2 lb. (225g) celery root, peeled and grated

1 carrot, peeled and grated

1 teaspoon lemon juice

1 tablespoon sesame oil or salad oil

4-6 green onions, finely chopped

1 teaspoon grated fresh ginger

Salt and pepper to taste

8 oz. (225g) fresh soft goat cheese

2 tablespoons toasted sesame seeds

1/4 lb. (115g) bean sprouts

1. Mix celery root, carrot, lemon juice and 1 teaspoon oil.

2. Add green onions, ginger, salt and pepper. Mix together and spoon into four individual ramekins, pressing down well. Turn onto four salad plates.

3. Mix soft goat cheese with a good grind of black pepper then shape into small balls and roll in toasted sesame seeds.

4. Toss bean sprouts in remaining oil and arrange around the molded salads. Top with cheese balls. Serve at once.

Makes 4 servings.

Each serving contains:

Cal	Prot	Carb	Fib	Tot. Fat	Sat. Fat	Chol	Sodium
247	14g	9g	4g	18g	9g	26mg	323mg

Chapter Five

STOVE-TOP DISHES

Recipes in this chapter are cooked in a single pan on top of the stove. I especially enjoy the convenience of one-pan dishes like Chile-Braised Cabbage, Braised Fennel with Rosemary and Olives, and Balaton Hotpot.

Omelets are very useful for quick meals and I have been experimenting with different fillings based on European and Middle Eastern cuisines. The results are quite spectacular, so do try them. I often serve these omelets when I have friends for supper. It's quicker to make one large omelet and cut it up than to make several individually cooked omelets.

I'm fond of combining sweet and savory flavors in the same dish. For example, coconut lends a special sweetness that doesn't overwhelm but complements other foods. Try Coconut Beans, Jamaican Run Down or Okra with Coconut and you'll see why I'm so enthusiastic about this ingredient.

WATERCRESS-AND-COTTAGE-CHEESE OMELET

Cottage cheese gives a light texture to this quickly made omelet and the watercress gives it an interesting spicy flavor.

4-5 tablespoons cottage cheese

1 clove garlic, crushed (optional)

1/2 bunch watercress, chopped

2 tablespoons grated fresh Parmesan cheese

1 tablespoon sunflower or safflower oil

6 eggs

6 tablespoons water

Salt and pepper to taste

1. Mix cottage cheese with garlic, if using, watercress and Parmesan cheese and set aside.
2. Heat oil in a large skillet. Beat eggs with water, salt and pepper and pour into skillet. Gently stir egg mixture so liquid egg flows beneath set egg. When omelet is lightly set, stop stirring to allow bottom to brown; top should remain creamy.
3. Dot with spoonfuls of cheese-and-watercress mixture. Fold in half and serve at once.

Makes 4 servings.

Each serving contains:

Cal	Prot	Carb	Fib	Tot. Fat	Sat. Fat	Chol	Sodium
173	13g	1g	0g	13g	4g	324mg	286mg

IRANIAN OMELET WITH ZUCCHINI AND MINT

Iranian omelets are flat like Spanish omelets, but they are not cooked for as long and should be just a little runny in the center. The yogurt makes them very light and fluffy.

Other combinations to use in place of zucchini and mint include peas and chopped fresh chervil, diced celeriac and chopped chives or green onions and chopped sage.

1/2 lb. (225g) zucchini, trimmed and diced

6 eggs, beaten

1/4 cup (60ml) plain yogurt

Salt and pepper to taste

2 tablespoons chopped fresh mint leaves

1 tablespoon cooking oil

1. Steam zucchini in a steamer or a little water for 4 minutes until tender.

2. Beat eggs with yogurt, salt, pepper and mint. Stir in cooked zucchini.

3. Heat oil in a small skillet and pour in egg mixture.

4. Cook over medium heat for 2 minutes, stir once or twice then cook another 6-8 minutes until just set in the center.

Makes 4 servings.

Each serving contains:

Cal	Prot	Carb	Fib	Tot. Fat	Sat. Fat	Chol	Sodium
177	12g	3g	1g	13g	3g	372mg	185mg

LEEK-AND-WALNUT OMELET

Inspiration for this omelet comes from the Middle East, where similar ingredients are sometimes baked in the oven to make large Spanish-style set omelets. I prefer my omelets to be a little runny in the center so I cook them on top of the stove and remove them from the heat just before they are fully set.

2 tablespoons (25g) butter

1 lb. (450g) leeks, trimmed and finely chopped

3/4 cup (75g) very coarsely chopped walnuts

6 eggs

1-1/2 teaspoons turmeric

Salt and pepper to taste

1. Heat 1 tablespoon butter in a skillet and add leeks and walnuts. Gently cook over low heat about 7 minutes until leeks are tender.

2. Transfer to a bowl, add other ingredients, except remaining butter, and beat.

3. Melt remaining butter in skillet. Pour in egg mixture and cook over medium heat 2-3 minutes, stirring gently once or twice. Fold omelet in half and serve.

Makes 4 servings.

Each serving contains:

Cal	Prot	Carb	Fib	Tot. Fat	Sat. Fat	Chol	Sodium
380	14g	22g	4g	28g	7g	334mg	245mg

SOUFFLÉ OMELET WITH SPINACH AND PINE NUTS

I wasn't sure whether to call this omelet *Florentine* because the main flavoring is spinach, and in Italy dishes using spinach are often so named, or *Roman* because the method of preparing the spinach comes from a friend in Rome. In the end I decided upon the longer but more descriptive name above!

1 tablespoon (15g) butter
2 tablespoons pine nuts
2 tablespoons raisins
1/4 teaspoon grated lemon peel
1 lb. (450g) fresh spinach, rinsed
6 eggs, separated
1/4 cup (60ml) water

1. Heat butter in a saucepan and gently sauté pine nuts, raisins and lemon peel until nuts begin to brown. Add spinach and toss over low heat until spinach begins to wilt. Chop coarsely and set aside to cool.

2. Beat egg yolks with water; add spinach mixture.

3. Whisk egg whites until very stiff. Stir 1 tablespoonful into egg-and-spinach mixture, then fold in the rest.

4. Pour into an ovenproof non-stick skillet and cook slowly over low heat 4-5 minutes. Preheat the broiler.

5. Place skillet under broiler and cook another 5 minutes until omelet is set in the center. Serve at once.

Makes 4 servings.

Each serving contains:

Cal	Prot	Carb	Fib.	Tot. Fat	Sat. Fat	Chol	Sodium
216	14g	10g	4g	15g	5g	327mg	219mg

GLAZED-GARLIC TOFU Ⓥ

This combination makes a well-flavored tofu to serve with almost any of the rice dishes given in Chapter 9. I sometimes vary the flavor by adding Chinese five-spice powder or toasted sesame seeds and fresh cilantro or coriander. Serve with plain boiled rice or fried noodles.

14-15 cloves garlic, peeled
1/4 teaspoon red-pepper flakes
3 tablespoons soy sauce
1/2 cup (125ml) vinegar
3 tablespoons honey
1/2 lb. (225g) fresh tofu

1. Blend garlic, pepper flakes, soy sauce, vinegar and honey in a food processor or blender. Transfer to a saucepan and cook, stirring occasionally, about 8 minutes until reduced by about one-third.

2. Meanwhile, cut tofu into thick strips or large cubes. Add to garlic-and-vinegar mixture and poach about 4 minutes until tofu is heated through.

Makes 4 servings.

Each serving contains:

Cal	Prot	Carb	Fib	Tot. Fat	Sat. Fat	Chol	Sodium
125	6g	23g	1g	3g	0g	0mg	993mg

CAULIFLOWER PROVENCE-STYLE Ⓥ

The rich, herby aromas of Provence come through powerfully in the sauce for this unusual method of preparing cauliflower. It makes a real change from cauliflower with cheese and is much faster to make.

1 tablespoon olive oil

2 cloves garlic, peeled, minced

1/4 teaspoon fennel seed (optional)

1 bay leaf

1 sprig fresh rosemary or
   1/4 teaspoon dried rosemary

2 tablespoons tomato purée

1/2 cup (125ml) vegetable stock,
   page 10

1 cauliflower, cut into large florets

6 black olives, pitted

Salt and pepper to taste

2 tablespoons chopped fresh
   parsley

1. Heat oil in a saucepan and gently sauté garlic, fennel seeds (if using), bay leaf and rosemary for about 1 minute.

2. Stir in tomato purée and stock. Add cauliflower, olives, salt and pepper and bring to a boil.

3. Cook over medium heat 10 minutes until the cauliflower is just tender, turning it in the juices occasionally.

4. Stir in parsley and serve.

Makes 4 servings.

Each serving contains:

Cal	Prot	Carb	Fib	Tot. Fat	Sat. Fat	Chol	Sodium
60	1g	5g	2g	4g	1g	0mg	178mg

CHILE-BRAISED CABBAGE

Treated carefully, cabbage forms the basis of a wide range of interesting dishes. This one comes from Hungary, where hot paprika is used. I used fresh green chile pepper to give the heat and sweet paprika for the flavor.

1 large onion, peeled and sliced

1 fresh green chile pepper, seeded and chopped

2 tablespoons olive oil

1/2 head white cabbage, shredded

4 large tomatoes, peeled and chopped

2 teaspoons paprika

1 teaspoon lime juice

1/3 cup (80ml) vegetable stock, page 10

Salt and pepper to taste

1. Sauté onion and chile pepper in oil 4-5 minutes until lightly browned. Add remaining ingredients and bring to a boil.

2. Cover and cook over medium heat 8 minutes, turning vegetables occasionally until tender.

Makes 4 servings.

Each serving contains:

Cal	Prot	Carb	Fib	Tot. Fat	Sat. Fat	Chol	Sodium
150	4g	20g	5g	8g	1g	0mg	107mg

SICILIAN POTATOES ⓥ

Serve this aromatic potato dish with a tossed green salad. Finish with a plate of aged Pecorino cheese and fresh pears, and you will immediately be transported to the sunny slopes of Mount Etna.

Capers are the pickled flower heads of the caper plant and they are used a great deal as a flavoring in Southern Italy. If you find them a little strong try the milder caper fruit which are beginning to appear on delicatessen shelves.

1 onion, peeled and sliced

1 tablespoon olive oil

1 can (28-oz. / 800g) tomatoes

16 black olives, pitted

1 tablespoon capers, rinsed and drained

1 tablespoon raisins

1 tablespoon pine nuts

2 tablespoons chopped fresh parsley

Salt and pepper to taste

2 lb. (900g) potatoes, peeled and cubed

1. Sauté onion in oil 4-5 minutes until lightly browned.

2. Using kitchen scissors chop tomatoes in the can, and add contents of can to the onion. Add remaining ingredients except potatoes. Bring to a boil.

3. Add potatoes, reduce heat and simmer 25 minutes, turning potatoes occasionally.

Makes 4 servings.

Each serving contains:

Cal	Prot	Carb	Fib	Tot. Fat	Sat. Fat	Chol	Sodium
323	7g	60g	6g	8g	1g	0mg	641mg

CALIFORNIA LIMA BEANS Ⓥ

This dish not only tastes delicious, it looks it too! Serve with stir-fried mixed vegetables and broccoli tossed with almonds for a really colorful spread. Finish this simple meal with a slice of pecan pie from your local bakery.

1 onion, peeled and finely chopped

2 cloves garlic, peeled and crushed

2 tablespoons olive oil

1 red bell pepper, finely chopped

1/4 lb. (115g) button mushrooms, finely chopped

1 can (14-oz. / 400g) chopped tomatoes

2 tablespoons tomato purée

1/4 teaspoon dried mixed Italian herbs

Salt and pepper to taste

1 can (15-oz. / 430g) lima beans, drained

1. Gently sauté onion and garlic in olive oil 2-3 minutes to soften them. Add bell pepper and mushrooms and cook 5 minutes, stirring frequently.

2. Add remaining ingredients except beans and continue cooking over low heat another 5 minutes. Add drained beans and cook 10-12 minutes until sauce thickens slightly.

Makes 4 servings.

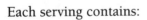

Each serving contains:

Cal	Prot	Carb	Fib	Tot. Fat	Sat. Fat	Chol	Sodium
210	8g	30g	7g	7g	1g	0mg	513mg

BRAISED FENNEL WITH ROSEMARY AND OLIVES Ⓥ

I came across this recipe, not in Provence or Tuscany as you might expect, but in New Orleans. It's surprising how strong the old European influences still are in some parts of that changing city. All the ingredients were available in the local market and the combination was the inspiration of an artist friend.

1/4 cup (60ml) extra-virgin olive oil

4 whole cloves garlic, peeled

8 small bulbs (about 2 lb. / 900g) fennel, trimmed to remove the fibrous outside layers, sliced

4 sprigs fresh rosemary or 1 teaspoon dried rosemary

12 black olives, pitted

1/4 cup (60ml) white wine

1. Heat oil in a shallow pan and sauté garlic cloves until lightly browned. Remove garlic from the pan and set aside.

2. Add fennel to oil and brown well on both sides.

3. Spread out over bottom of pan. Add rosemary, olives and wine, and bring to a boil.

4. Cover pan, reduce heat and cook gently for 20 minutes until fennel is cooked and most liquid has evaporated. Boil off excess liquid. Serve with reserved garlic cloves, if desired.

Makes 4 servings.

Each serving contains:

Cal	Prot	Carb	Fib	Tot. Fat	Sat. Fat	Chol	Sodium
290	6g	35g	20g	16g	2g	0mg	362mg

BEANS PROVENÇALE Ⓥ

This recipe was inspired by a dish of braised celery I was served in a small restaurant just outside the amphitheater at Orange in Provence. It's so good I sometimes serve the dish as a course on its own.

1 tablespoon (15g) butter

2 shallots or 4 green onions, finely chopped

1 clove garlic, peeled and crushed

Pinch of fennel seeds

Pinch of dried rosemary

Pinch of dried thyme

3 tomatoes, peeled, seeded and chopped

1 lb. (450g) fresh green beans

1/2 cup (125ml) vegetable stock, page 10

Salt and pepper to taste

1. Melt butter in a pan and gently sauté shallots or green onions, garlic, fennel seeds and dried herbs for 1 minute.
2. Add tomatoes, beans, stock, salt and pepper. Simmer over gentle heat 10-12 minutes, shaking the pan occasionally. Beans should be tender-crisp.

Makes 4 servings.

Each serving contains:

Cal	Prot	Carb	Fib	Tot. Fat	Sat. Fat	Chol	Sodium
89	3g	15g	6g	3g	2g	8mg	115mg

CHICKPEAS WITH SPINACH Ⓥ

Chickpeas or garbanzos, as they are also known, are very popular in the tapas bars of Seville, Spain. This dish is usually served in an oval dish surrounded by triangles of bread fried in olive oil.

1 clove garlic, peeled and crushed

1 small onion, peeled and chopped

2 tablespoons olive oil

A few strands of saffron (optional)

3 tomatoes, skinned, seeded and chopped

1 can (14-oz. / 400g) chickpeas or garbanzos, drained

1 lb. (450g) spinach, washed and shredded

1. Sauté garlic and onion in oil until softened. Add saffron, if using, and cook a minute longer. Add tomatoes and cook another 2-3 minutes to make a thick paste. Add chickpeas or garbanzos and mix well.

2. Cook spinach in a covered pan without any water 1-2 minutes until crisp-tender.

3. Toss spinach with chickpeas or garbanzos and spoon into a bowl to serve.

Makes 4 servings.

Each serving contains:

Cal	Prot	Carb	Fib	Tot. Fat	Sat. Fat	Chol	Sodium
203	8g	251g	10g	10g	1g	0mg	312mg

BALATON HOTPOT

The inspiration for this filling winter warmer is part Hungarian and part Turkish. The combination is not unusual in Eastern Europe, where the legacy of the Turkish occupation in the late eighteenth century has had quite an impact on culinary traditions. Rice, of course, is the Turkish contribution and the dish is often made with meat or poultry as well as beans.

1 onion, peeled and chopped

2 tablespoons vegetable oil

1 cup (75g) long-grain rice

1 large potato (9 oz. / 250g), peeled, cubed

1/4 teaspoon caraway seeds

1-2 teaspoons strong paprika

1 tablespoon tomato purée

3 tablespoons sour cream

1 cup (250ml) water

Salt and pepper to taste

1 can (6 oz. / 175g) red kidney or haricot beans, well drained

1. Gently sauté onion in oil until lightly browned. Add rice and cook a minute longer. Add potato cubes.

2. Meanwhile, combine remaining ingredients except beans.

3. Pour sour cream mixture over rice and vegetables and bring to a boil. Reduce heat and cover. Simmer 20 minutes. Add beans and cook another 5-8 minutes until potatoes and rice are tender.

Makes 4 servings.

Each serving contains:

Cal	Prot	Carb	Fib	Tot. Fat	Sat. Fat	Chol	Sodium
255	6g	37g	5g	10g	2g	5mg	94mg

CREOLE EGGS

I like this dish served with crusty whole-wheat bread, but it can also be served with boiled rice or mashed potatoes, both of which will take about the same amount of time to cook as the eggs.

8 eggs

1 tablespoon vegetable oil

2 medium onions, peeled and sliced

1 green bell pepper, seeded and sliced

1 red bell pepper, seeded and sliced

2 tablespoons cornstarch

1-1/2 cups (375ml) milk

4 medium tomatoes, quartered

Salt and pepper to taste

1/4 cup (60ml) chopped fresh parsley

1. Cook eggs in simmering water 10-12 minutes. Drain them and rinse in cold water.

2. Heat oil in a large saucepan and gently sauté onions and bell peppers for 5 minutes.

3. Mix cornstarch with a little of the milk to make a smooth paste. Mix in remaining milk and pour over vegetables. Stirring constantly, bring to a boil. When mixture thickens add tomatoes, salt and pepper.

4. Reduce heat, cover and simmer 5-6 minutes, stirring occasionally.

5. Meanwhile, peel eggs and cut in half lengthwise.

6. Add eggs and half the parsley to sauce. Stir gently, then cook another 3 minutes.

7. Pour into a serving dish and sprinkle with remaining parsley.

Makes 4 servings.

Each serving contains:

Cal	Prot	Carb	Fib	Tot. Fat	Sat. Fat	Chol	Sodium
298	18g	22g	3g	16g	5g	432mg	254mg

MOROCCAN TAGINE OF SWISS CHARD ⓥ

Tagine is both the North African word for stew and the name of the earthenware dish in which stews are frequently cooked. All kinds of ingredients find their way into a tagine, the inspiration coming from the state of the larder. This recipe comes from the Tehian area of Morocco, where it is often served with a simple dish of stewed lentils. Swiss chard has spinach-type leaves with a wide stalk. Use both the leaves and the stalks for this dish.

2 lb. (1kg) Swiss chard

2 onions, peeled and chopped

1/4 cup (60ml) chopped fresh cilantro or coriander

3 tablespoons rice

6 tablespoons vegetable stock, page 10, or water

1/4 cup (60ml) olive oil

1 teaspoon paprika

Salt and pepper to taste

1. Wash Swiss chard and dry well on paper towels. Chop finely.

2. Place all ingredients in a saucepan and bring to a boil.

3. Reduce heat and simmer 15 minutes until vegetables and rice are tender and mixture is thickened.

Each serving contains:

Cal	Prot	Carb	Fib	Tot. Fat	Sat. Fat	Chol	Sodium
218	5g	21g	5g	14g	2g	0mg	553mg

TAGINE OF OKRA AND TOMATOES Ⓥ

Choose small okra for this dish, which comes from the same area of Morocco as the Moroccan Tagine of Swiss Chard, page 96. Take care not to overcook the okra as it can be very glutinous and stringy if it starts to break up. Serve with rice.

2 lb. (1kg) ripe tomatoes, peeled, seeded and chopped

2 tablespoons chopped fresh parsley

2 teaspoons paprika

1 clove garlic, peeled and crushed

Salt and pepper to taste

3 tablespoons olive oil

1/2 lb. (225g) fresh okra

1. Place all ingredients except okra in a saucepan. Bring to a boil and cook 10 minutes, stirring constantly, until tomatoes have broken down and mixture is fairly thick.

2. Reduce heat and add okra, pushing it down into the sauce. Cover and continue to simmer 10 minutes until okra is cooked.

Makes 4 servings.

Each serving contains:

Cal	Prot	Carb	Fib	Tot. Fat	Sat. Fat	Chol	Sodium
160	3g	16g	4g	11g	2g	0mg	91mg

JAMAICAN RUN DOWN ⓥ

I don't know how this fragrant dish got its name but it seems to be a use-anything-on-hand kind of vegetable stew. The coconut and sweet potatoes complement each other well but they do need the regular potatoes to provide a balance. Otherwise you can use almost any kind of vegetables you have on hand.

*1 can (14 oz. / 400ml) unsweet-
ened coconut milk*

3/4 cup (185ml) water

1 small onion, peeled and chopped

2 carrots, peeled and diced

1 green bell pepper, seeded, diced

1 bay leaf

*2 sprigs fresh thyme or
1/4 teaspoon dried thyme*

1 clove garlic, peeled and chopped

*1 green chile pepper, seeded,
chopped*

2 potatoes, peeled, diced

2 sweet potatoes, peeled, diced

*1 can (4 oz. / 125g) kidney beans,
drained*

1 teaspoon soy sauce

1. In a large pan, bring coconut milk and water to a boil, stirring frequently.

2. Add onion, carrots, bell pepper, bay leaf, thyme, garlic and chile pepper and return to a boil. Reduce heat and simmer, uncovered, 10 minutes.

3. Add potatoes and sweet potatoes, return to a boil, reduce heat and simmer 18 minutes until vegetables are tender.

4. Add beans and soy sauce and cook another 2-3 minutes to heat through. If the mixture is very thin, increase heat and boil rapidly to reduce.

Makes 4 servings.

Each serving contains:

Cal	Prot	Carb	Fib	Tot. Fat	Sat. Fat	Chol	Sodium
462	12g	60g	14g	22g	20g	0mg	150mg

OKRA WITH COCONUT Ⓥ

This is quite a dry dish from Southern India. Choose the smallest and youngest okra pods that you can find as they will be much more tender and far less stringy and gelatinous than larger, older ones. Look for tiny baby okra less than an inch (1-2cm) long, and use them in this delicious way.

2 tablespoons corn oil

1/4 teaspoon whole yellow
   mustard seeds

Seeds from 3 cardamom pods

1 small onion, peeled and minced

1/2 teaspoon turmeric

1/2 lb. (225g) okra, sliced across
   the pods

3 tablespoons (15g) shredded
   coconut

Salt to taste

GARNISH

Chopped fresh cilantro or
   coriander leaves

1. Heat oil in a pan and sauté mustard and cardamom seeds until they pop. Add onion and sauté for 1-2 minutes.

2. Add remaining ingredients and cook 6-8 minutes longer, stirring constantly, until the okra is tender but still retains its shape. Serve garnished with chopped cilantro or coriander.

Makes 4 servings.

Each serving contains:

Cal	Prot	Carb	Fib	Tot. Fat	Sat. Fat	Chol	Sodium
113	2g	7g	3g	9g	3g	0mg	72mg

CURRIED BEANS

This straightforward curry is fairly mild, so if you like your curries hot add a few drops of Tabasco sauce. Serve with a vegetable curry and spiced rice or potatoes sautéed with cardamom.

3 large cloves garlic, peeled and chopped

1 piece (2-inch / 5cm) fresh ginger, peeled and chopped

1 large onion, peeled and chopped

1 teaspoon cumin seeds

1 teaspoon coriander seeds

Seeds from 4 cardamom pods

2 cloves

3 tablespoons cooking oil

1 tablespoon ground cumin

2 tablespoons ground coriander

1 can (14-oz. / 400g) blackeyed beans, drained

1 can (7-oz. / 200g) lima beans, drained

1/2 lb. (225g) fresh green beans, sliced

2 tablespoons ground almonds

1/2 cup (125g) plain yogurt

1/2 cup (125ml) vegetable stock, page 10, or water

1. Purée garlic, ginger and onion in a food processor or blender and set aside.

2. Sauté cumin, coriander and cardamom seeds and cloves in cooking oil for about 1 minute until they start to pop. Take care not to burn them.

3. Remove from heat and discard cloves. Stir in ground spices and garlic-onion purée.

4. Return to heat and add remaining ingredients. Stir and bring to a boil. Reduce heat, cover and simmer 15 minutes.

Makes 4 servings.

Each serving contains:

Cal	Prot	Carb	Fib	Tot. Fat	Sat. Fat	Chol	Sodium
277	11g	33g	8g	14g	2g	2mg	339mg

COCONUT BEANS Ⓥ

This dish appeals to both the eye and the tastebuds. Serve with Lentil Burgers, page 116, and rice.

1 clove garlic, peeled and crushed

1 tablespoon cooking oil

1/2 lb. (225g) shelled fresh lima beans

4 oz. (115g) frozen green beans, thawed

2 tablespoons chopped fresh parsley

3 tablespoons chopped fresh basil

2 tablespoons sliced green onion

1 cup (250ml) unsweetened coconut milk

2 tablespoons dry sherry

2 teaspoons lemon juice

GARNISH

Fresh basil leaves

1. Sauté garlic in oil for 1 minute and then add remaining ingredients except lemon juice.
2. Bring to a boil, reduce heat and simmer 5 minutes until vegetables are tender. Add lemon juice and serve at once, garnished with basil.

Makes 4 servings.

Each serving contains:

Cal	Prot	Carb	Fib	Tot. Fat	Sat. Fat	Chol	Sodium
219	5g	15g	4g	16g	11g	0mg	16mg

Chapter Six

GRILLS AND BARBECUES

R ecipes in this chapter range from simple grilled vegetables with interesting sauces to burgers and kebabs. People often think that a vegetarian barbecue is difficult to manage, but most vegetables grill very well. You can also use tofu and cheeses which do not start to run when heated, such as Halloumi and feta.

Most of these recipes can be cooked in a variety of ways. Depending on your equipment, they can be barbecued, grilled or broiled.

Many times I enlist the help of my family or guests in preparing these meals. They especially enjoy taking charge of the barbecue and overseeing a simple recipe like Grilled Zucchini with Walnut Mayonnaise or Grilled Eggplant with Moroccan Sauce.

GRILLED ZUCCHINI WITH WALNUT MAYONNAISE

The best kind of mayonnaise is homemade but if you do not have the time or the inclination to make your own you can use a prepared mayonnaise for this recipe. However you will have to be careful with the amount of walnut oil that you add. I found that 1/4 cup of oil blends perfectly with 1/4 cup prepared mayonnaise.

4-6 large zucchini, trimmed and thickly sliced lengthwise

5-6 tablespoons walnut oil

Salt and pepper to taste

1/4 cup mayonnaise

1 tablespoon chopped walnuts

1. Preheat grill. Brush zucchini slices with 1 tablespoon walnut oil. Sprinkle with salt and pepper.

2. Grill zucchini 2-3 minutes on each side until tender and lightly charred.

3. Meanwhile, beat remaining walnut oil and walnuts into mayonnaise with a whisk. Serve with grilled zucchini.

Makes 4 servings.

Each serving contains:

Cal	Prot	Carb	Fib	Tot. Fat	Sat. Fat	Chol	Sodium
323	3g	7g	3g	33g	4g	8mg	152mg

GRILLED VEGETABLES WITH PESTO MAYONNAISE

Many vegetables, such as sliced fennel, endive, baby carrots and baby corn, can be used in this recipe. Start cooking the hardest vegetables first as they take the longest to cook. Semi-cooked vegetables can be transferred from the grill rack to the base of the pan as cooking continues. In this way you should be able to prepare enough for four people as a starter, or two as a main course.

1 sweet potato, scrubbed and sliced

1 eggplant, trimmed and sliced

2 tablespoons olive oil

1 red bell pepper, seeded and cut into 8 pieces

2 zucchini, trimmed and sliced lengthwise

1/4 cup (60ml) mayonnaise

1-2 teaspoons pesto sauce

Sprigs of fresh parsley

Sprigs of fresh chervil, tarragon or basil

1. Preheat grill. Brush sweet potato and eggplant slices on both sides with oil. Grill until lightly browned, 2-3 minutes on each side. Set aside and cover.

2. Brush bell pepper and zucchini with remaining oil and place on rack. Grill about 3 minutes or until peppers are well charred. Turn zucchini slices over once during this time.

3. Meanwhile, combine mayonnaise and pesto sauce.

4. Arrange vegetables on serving plates, garnish with fresh herbs. Serve with pesto mayonnaise.

Makes 4 servings.

Each serving contains:

Cal	Prot	Carb	Fib	Tot. Fat	Sat. Fat	Chol	Sodium
222	2g	12g	3g	19g	3g	9mg	102mg

Opposite: Egg-and-Zucchini Bake, page 52

ITALIAN MARINATED VEGETABLES Ⓥ

Italians are fond of vegetable antipasto dishes like this one, made by simply marinating grilled vegetables in flavored olive oil.

1 red bell pepper, seeded and quartered

1 yellow or orange bell pepper, seeded and quartered

2-3 zucchini, trimmed and sliced lengthwise

1 small eggplant, cut into rings

2/3 cup (160ml) extra-virgin olive oil

1 clove garlic, peeled and crushed

1 tablespoon chopped fresh tarragon or 1 teaspoon dried tarragon

1 tablespoon chopped fresh parsley

GARNISH
Black olives

1. Preheat grill. Grill vegetables until they begin to char.

2. Put bell peppers into a plastic bag and tie. Set aside for 15 minutes and then peel off charred skins. Arrange vegetables in a shallow dish.

3. Mix remaining ingredients and pour over vegetables. Let stand for as long as possible before serving. Serve garnished with black olives.

Makes 4 servings.

Each serving contains:

Cal	Prot	Carb	Fib	Tot. Fat	Sat. Fat	Chol	Sodium
400	3g	17g	6g	38g	5g	0mg	87mg

Opposite: Cheese-and-Bean Rosti, page 61

GRILLED EGGPLANT WITH MOROCCAN SAUCE Ⓥ

The warmth of the grilled eggplant brings out all the flavors in this piquant sauce from North Africa. Serve on its own as a first course for the best effect. Follow with a tagine or couscous.

2 large eggplants, trimmed and
    thickly sliced

Olive oil for brushing

MOROCCAN SAUCE

1/4 cup (60ml) olive oil

1 clove garlic, peeled and crushed

1 teaspoon grated fresh ginger

1 green chile pepper, seeded and
    chopped

1/2 teaspoon ground cumin

1/4 cup (60ml) chopped fresh
    cilantro or coriander

1 tablespoon lemon juice

Salt and pepper to taste

1. Preheat grill to medium hot. Brush eggplant slices with oil and grill 3-4 minutes until lightly browned. Turn slices over. Grill another 3-4 minutes until lightly browned and cooked through.

2. Place sauce ingredients in a food processor or blender and mix together.

3. Arrange eggplant on four warmed plates and top with sauce. Serve at once.

Makes 4 servings.

Each serving contains:

Cal	Prot	Carb	Fib	Tot. Fat	Sat. Fat	Chol	Sodium
319	2g	19g	7g	28g	4g	0mg	75mg

BROILED MUSHROOMS WITH PESTO SAUCE

This is one of the fastest hot dishes I know. As well as being an excellent starter it can be served with any of the rice dishes in Chapter 9.

8 portobello mushrooms
1/2 cup (50g) prepared pesto sauce
Freshly ground black pepper

1. Preheat broiler to medium hot. Clean mushrooms with a damp paper towel. Remove stems and and spread pesto sauce over gills (undersides).
2. Broil 5-6 minutes until done as desired.

Makes 4 servings.

Each serving contains:

Cal	Prot	Carb	Fib	Tot. Fat	Sat. Fat	Chol	Sodium
133	7g	12g	3g	8g	2g	4mg	112mg

BROILED MUSHROOMS WITH SALSA Ⓥ

I like the spicy flavor of this Mexican salsa. I have never come across mushrooms served with salsa in any Mexican cookbook but the combination works very well.

8 portobello mushrooms

Olive oil for brushing

Salt and pepper to taste

1-2 cloves garlic, peeled and crushed (optional)

SALSA

1 lb. (450g) yellow tomatoes, finely chopped

1 tablespoon grated lime peel

Juice of 1 lime

6-8 green onions, chopped

6 tablespoons chopped fresh cilantro or coriander

1 green chile pepper, seeded and chopped

1. Combine salsa ingredients in a bowl and refrigerate while finishing the recipe.
2. Preheat broiler. Clean mushrooms with a damp paper towel and remove stems. Brush mushrooms all over with oil and sprinkle with salt, pepper and garlic, if using.
3. Broil mushrooms 4-5 minutes depending on thickness. Brush with more oil if necessary.
4. When mushrooms are cooked, top with salsa and return to broiler to warm.

Makes 4 servings.

Each serving contains:

Cal	Prot	Carb	Fib	Tot. Fat	Sat. Fat	Chol	Sodium
215	6g	20g	5g	15g	2g	0mg	90mg

GRILLED FETA CHEESE WITH OLIVES

A dish I had in a Greek restaurant was the inspiration for this new favorite. Rain was streaming down the windows and the temperature was way below anything you might experience in Greece. I wanted something hot and Grilled Cheese with Olives was the answer—plus a large glass of ouzo!

8 oz. (225g) feta cheese
6 tablespoons olive oil
2 pita loaves, split in two
Grated peel and juice of 1/2 lemon
Freshly ground black pepper
24 black olives, pitted and halved
Pinch of dried thyme

1. Preheat broiler to medium hot. Cut cheese into thick slices and brush with olive oil.

2. Toast pita bread lightly on both sides and top with cheese slices. Broil a few minutes. Transfer to four serving plates.

3. In a saucepan, warm remaining oil with lemon peel and juice and black pepper; do not allow to boil.

4. Sprinkle olives over cheese toasts and top with flavored olive oil. Sprinkle with thyme and serve at once.

Makes 4 servings.

Each serving contains:

Cal	Prot	Carb	Fib	Tot. Fat	Sat. Fat	Chol	Sodium
434	13g	17g	3g	36g	12g	51mg	983mg

BANANA KEBABS Ⓥ

Sorrel is beginning to appear in the supermarkets nowadays and its tangy sharp flavor goes very well with bananas. If I cannot find sorrel I use arugula, but the flavor is not quite as good. Serve with rice or bulgur for a main course.

8 ears of baby corn
12 sorrel leaves, stalks removed
3 large bananas, peeled and each cut into 4 pieces
12 cherry tomatoes
Salt and pepper to taste

1. Place baby corn in a pan of boiling water and cook 10 minutes. Drain.

2. Meanwhile, plunge sorrel leaves into boiling water. Remove immediately and plunge into cold water. Drain.

3. Wrap sorrel leaves around banana pieces and thread onto skewers with corn and cherry tomatoes.

4. Season with salt and pepper and broil or grill 6-8 minutes, turning frequently.

Makes 4 servings.

Each serving contains:

Cal	Prot	Carb	Fib	Tot. Fat	Sat. Fat	Chol	Sodium
100	2g	24g	3g	1g	0g	0mg	78mg

TOFU SKEWERS IN PEANUT-BUTTER MARINADE ⓥ

This peanut-butter marinade has a surprisingly delicate flavor. If you like a stronger flavor, add a teaspoonful or two of soy sauce. Serve with rice or bulgur for a main course.

2 tablespoons peanut butter
1 clove garlic, peeled and crushed
Juice of 1 lemon
2 tablespoons water
8 oz. (225g) tofu
3 green bell peppers, seeded and cut into quarters

1. Mix peanut butter, garlic, lemon juice and water to make a pouring consistency.
2. Cut tofu into eight squares and marinate in peanut butter mixture for 20 minutes.
3. Preheat broiler. Blanch bell peppers by placing in boiling water for 3 minutes. Drain and thread onto skewers with tofu.
4. Place kebabs under the hot broiler and cook about 6 minutes, turning and basting with the remaining marinade.

Makes 4 servings.

Each serving contains:

Cal	Prot	Carb	Fib	Tot. Fat	Sat. Fat	Chol	Sodium
110	7g	8g	2g	7g	1g	0mg	43mg

ONION-AND-MUSHROOM KEBABS Ⓥ

For an even speedier version of this recipe I use roasted baby onions packed in olive oil and marinated whole mushrooms. The roasted onions come from Spain or Italy, but I prepare the marinated mushrooms myself. I cook them as in step 1 below, then pack them in olive oil for later use. However you can still make the kebabs in half an hour using raw onions and mushrooms.

1/2 lb. (225g) small boiling onions

1/2 lb. (225g) large button mushrooms

1/2 cup (125ml) white wine

1 tablespoon tomato purée

1/2 teaspoon fennel or celery seeds

1 bay leaf

1 large red bell pepper, seeded and cut into quarters

2 tablespoons olive oil

Salt and pepper to taste

1. Preheat broiler or grill. Place onions, mushrooms, wine, tomato purée, fennel or celery seeds and bay leaf in a saucepan and bring to a boil. Cover and simmer 5-8 minutes to soften onions.

2. Grill bell pepper for a minute or two but do not char. Cut into smaller pieces.

3. Thread onions, mushrooms and peppers onto skewers and brush with oil. Season to taste.

4. Place under broiler or over grill and cook 5-6 minutes until lightly charred, turning occasionally.

Makes 4 servings.

Each serving contains:

Cal	Prot	Carb	Fib	Tot. Fat	Sat. Fat	Chol	Sodium
126	2g	10g	2g	7g	1g	0mg	219mg

HALLOUMI CHEESE WITH BALSAMIC VINEGAR

Halloumi cheese can be found in Greek and Arab food markets. The longer you soak the raisins in the balsamic vinegar mixture the better the flavor will be. Serve with rice and a stir-fry dish from Chapter 7.

3 tablespoons raisins

1 tablespoon lemon juice

1 teaspoon balsamic vinegar

8 oz. (225g) Halloumi cheese, cut into 4 thick slices

Mixed salad greens

2 tablespoons toasted pine nuts

Extra-virgin olive oil

1. Preheat broiler. Place raisins in a bowl with lemon juice and balsamic vinegar and set aside.

2. Broil cheese on both sides 4-5 minutes until golden all over.

3. Arrange salad greens on four plates and place cheese on top.

4. Spoon raisins and their juices over cheese and top with toasted pine nuts.

5. Drizzle with olive oil and serve at once.

Makes 4 servings.

Each serving contains:

Cal	Prot	Carb	Fib	Tot. Fat	Sat. Fat	Chol	Sodium
290	13g	10g	2g	24g	9g	44mg	233mg

CURRIED TOFU WITH CHUTNEY

Here's my version of an unusual Far-Eastern chutney.

8 oz. (225g) tofu
1/4 cup (60ml) plain yogurt
2 cloves garlic, peeled and crushed
1 tablespoon grated fresh ginger
2-3 teaspoons mild curry powder
1 tablespoon olive oil

CHUTNEY
1 dried red chile pepper
1/2 small onion, peeled and finely grated
2 tablespoons cooking oil
2 teaspoons turmeric
3 cups (250g) shredded moist coconut
2-3 sprigs fresh mint, chopped
5-6 tablespoons lemon juice

1. Cut tofu into 4 thick strips and place on a plate. Combine, yogurt, garlic, ginger, curry powder and olive oil and spoon over the tofu. Let stand, turning tofu occasionally, until needed. Preheat grill or broiler.

2. To make chutney: Slice chile pepper lengthwise, remove seeds and discard. Mince pepper. Sauté with onion in oil until soft. Add turmeric and cook another 2 minutes.

3. Add coconut and mint and toss together well. Cook another 4 minutes, add lemon juice and toss. Remove from heat and set aside.

4. Grill or broil tofu strips 4-5 minutes on each side. Serve with chutney.

Makes 4 servings.

Each serving contains:

Cal	Prot	Carb	Fib	Tot. Fat	Sat. Fat	Chol	Sodium
394	8g	18g	8g	35g	21g	2mg	27mg

MUSHROOM-AND-TOFU BURGERS

Vegetable-based burgers taste much better if they are crisp on the outside and moist on the inside. To achieve this I always use fresh vegetables in the mix and grate or chop them finely so they cook evenly.

6 oz. (175g) carrots, peeled and grated

1/4 lb. (115g) mushrooms, minced

1 onion, peeled and minced

1 clove garlic, peeled and crushed

8 oz. (225g) tofu

3/4 cup (115g) fresh whole-wheat breadcrumbs

Salt and pepper to taste

1 oz. (25g) chopped fresh cilantro or coriander leaves

1 oz. (25g) chopped fresh parsley

Cooking oil

Warm sesame buns

SAUCE

2 tablespoons tahini paste

2 tablespoons plain yogurt

Juice of 1 lemon

1 teaspoon sesame oil

1. Preheat grill or broiler. Combine vegetables and garlic in a bowl.

2. Mash tofu with a fork and add to vegetables. Add remaining burger ingredients except oil and buns. Mix well.

3. Shape into eight flat burgers and brush with oil. Grill or broil 5 minutes on each side, brushing occasionally with oil.

4. Combine sauce ingredients, adding a little water if the mixture is too thick. Serve with burgers on sesame buns.

Makes 4 servings.

Each serving contains:

Cal	Prot	Carb	Fib	Tot. Fat	Sat. Fat	Chol	Sodium
359	13g	40g	5g	18g	3g	1mg	392mg

LENTIL BURGERS ⓥ

My father is an excellent cook and this is one of his specialties. The burgers are crispy on the outside and light and soft in the center. He was rather vague about quantities, but after a couple of testing sessions I achieved the right results.

1/4 lb. (115g) red or yellow split lentils

1/2 lb. (225g) button mushrooms, chopped

1 cup (250ml) vegetable stock, page 10

Pinch of mixed dried herbs

Salt and pepper to taste

3 tablespoons millet or oat flakes

Cooking oil

1. Place all ingredients except the millet or oat flakes and cooking oil in a saucepan and bring to a boil. Cover and cook for 20 minutes. Preheat broiler.

2. Mash contents of pan, which should be fairly dry, and shape into eight flat burgers. Coat with millet or oat flakes.

3. Brush burgers with oil and place on a piece of foil. Broil 3 minutes on each side.

Makes 4 servings.

Each serving contains:

Cal	Prot	Carb	Fib	Tot. Fat	Sat. Fat	Chol	Sodium
190	10g	23g	5g	7g	1g	0mg	75mg

EGGPLANT WITH OLIVE PASTE AND TOMATOES Ⓥ

This is one of the best recipes I know for a quick-and-easy hot after-work starter. Its rich southern Italian flavors never fail to perk up the taste buds and the spirits. I sometimes add a slice of mozzarella or goat cheese to each slice of eggplant just before removing from the grill.

2 eggplants, trimmed and cut into 16 thick slices

Olive oil

1 jar (4-oz. / 115g) black-olive paste

4 tomatoes, each cut into 4 thick slices

Freshly ground black pepper

·1. Preheat grill or broiler to medium hot. Lightly brush eggplant slices with olive oil and grill 2-3 minutes on each side, until golden brown in color and cooked through.

2. Spread eggplant slices with olive paste. Top with tomato slices and season with pepper.

3. Return to heat and cook another 1-2 minutes. Serve at once.

Makes 4 servings.

Each serving contains:

Cal	Prot	Carb	Fib	Tot. Fat	Sat. Fat	Chol	Sodium
193	4g	25g	9g	11g	1g	0mg	266mg

Chapter Seven

WOK COOKERY

Stir-frying is a very quick method of cooking. It is important to get the wok as hot as possible before adding the food. A non-stick wok is useful for some dishes but not essential. If you do not have a wok you can use a deep-sided skillet, preferably with rounded sides. However, be careful to keep the food moving and to prevent it from sticking to the sides.

You do not need to use very much oil for stir-frying—the temptation is to add too much. If the ingredients seem to be too dry or if they start to burn during cooking, add a tablespoon of stock, wine or water and then stir-fry over medium to high heat.

The length of time needed to stir-fry particular vegetables depends on how crisp you like them to be. My preference is to have root vegetables, asparagus and beans a little softer than items such as cabbage, bean sprouts and sugar peas—those tender little edible peapods.

STIR-FRIED EGGS WITH BROCCOLI

Stir-fried eggs are more like scrambled eggs than an omelet, but they should not be too broken up. The method is used in both China and Italy. In the former the eggs are served with egg noodles and in the latter with pasta—take your pick.

1 lb. (450g) broccoli, cut into pieces, stems peeled

1/2 cup (125ml) vegetable stock, page 10

1/4 green bell pepper, seeded and diced

1/4 red bell pepper, seeded and diced

2 tablespoons chopped green onion

2 tablespoons cooking oil

4 eggs, beaten

2 tablespoons water

Salt and pepper to taste

1. Cook broccoli in boiling vegetable stock 3-4 minutes. Drain.

2. Meanwhile, sauté bell peppers and green onions in oil in a non-stick skillet or wok for about 2 minutes.

3. Mix eggs, water, salt and pepper and pour over the top. Stir-fry for about 30 seconds. As eggs begin to set, add broccoli, stir and serve at once.

Makes 4 servings.

Each serving contains:

Cal	Prot	Carb	Fib	Tot. Fat	Sat. Fat	Chol	Sodium
173	10g	8g	4g	12g	3g	213mg	163mg

STIR-FRIED EGGS WITH BEANS AND PEPPERS

This stir-fried egg dish is fresh and crunchy as well as creamy! For a different look use a yellow or orange bell pepper.

4 eggs, beaten

1 tablespoon milk

2 tablespoons chopped fresh parsley

Salt and pepper to taste

Butter

1 tablespoon cooking oil

2 leeks, trimmed and minced

1 red bell pepper, seeded and chopped

1 pkg. (10-oz. / 280g) frozen lima beans, thawed

1 tablespoon soy sauce

2 tablespoons vegetable stock, page 10, or water

1 tablespoon sherry

1. Mix eggs with milk, parsley, salt and pepper.

2. Heat butter in a non-stick wok or deep skillet and add eggs. Stir eggs so they do not set into a solid mass but do not scramble them.

3. When eggs are set, transfer to a plate and keep warm.

4. Clean pan with a paper towel and add oil. Stir-fry leeks, bell pepper and beans 2-3 minutes. Add remaining ingredients.

5. Continue to stir-fry over high heat until liquid has almost evaporated and beans are cooked. Return eggs to pan, toss well and serve at once.

Makes 4 servings.

Each serving contains:

Cal	Prot	Carb	Fib	Tot. Fat	Sat. Fat	Chol	Sodium
252	12g	25g	7g	12g	4g	221mg	542mg

TOFU WITH MUSHROOMS Ⓥ

Depending on the brand of chile bean paste that you use, this can be quite a spicy dish. I usually choose a Szechwan black-bean sauce, which is pretty hot. Serve with rice for a main course.

1-1/2 cups (375ml) cooking oil plus 1 tablespoon

1 lb. (450g) tofu, cubed

1-1/2 tablespoons minced garlic

2 teaspoons minced fresh ginger

2 green onions, trimmed and cut in half lengthwise

1/4 lb. (115g) button mushrooms

2 teaspoons chile bean paste

1-1/2 tablespoons dry sherry

1 tablespoon soy sauce

1 teaspoon salt

1/2 teaspoon freshly ground black pepper

2 tablespoons vegetable stock, page 10, or water

1. Heat 1-1/2 cups oil in a deep-fryer or a large wok until hot and smoking. Deep-fry tofu in batches until lightly browned. Drain on paper towels.

2. Heat another wok or skillet. Add remaining 1 tablespoon oil, garlic, ginger and green onions. Stir-fry a few seconds, then add mushrooms. Stir-fry for 30 seconds; add remaining ingredients except tofu.

3. Reduce heat to very low and add tofu. Cover and simmer about 8 minutes.

Makes 4 servings.

Each serving contains:

Cal	Prot	Carb	Fib	Tot. Fat	Sat. Fat	Chol	Sodium
198	10g	6g	2g	16g	2g	0mg	875mg

TOFU-TOPPED MUSHROOMS Ⓥ

This well-flavored stir-fry will please anyone who likes Chinese food. Tofu and mushrooms are both enlivened with garlic.

4 large or 8 small mushrooms

2 tablespoons cooking oil

2 tablespoons sesame cooking oil

8 whole cloves garlic, peeled

1/2 tablespoon grated fresh ginger

6-8 green onions, trimmed and cut into 1-inch (2.5cm) lengths

1/4 teaspoon grated orange peel

2 tablespoons soy sauce

1/2 lb. (225g) fresh tofu, cut into cubes

1. Preheat broiler. Trim mushroom stems. Brush mushrooms with oil and broil about 5 minutes on each side or until the mushrooms begin to soften.

2. Place sesame oil in a non-stick wok or deep skillet and gently sauté garlic for 5 minutes to soften it.

3. Add ginger and green onions and stir-fry for 30 seconds. Add orange peel, soy sauce and tofu cubes and toss over high heat until mixed. Spoon over mushrooms and serve at once with boiled rice.

Makes 4 servings.

Each serving contains:

Cal	Prot	Carb	Fib	Tot. Fat	Sat. Fat	Chol	Sodium
226	10g	13g	4g	17g	2g	0mg	672mg

BRAISED SPICY EGGPLANT Ⓥ

The Chinese have always used their woks to braise food as well as to stir-fry it. Braising usually involves more sauce than would be used in stir-frying and a certain amount of reduction takes place. The results can be quite rich and spicy. Serve with rice or noodles.

2 tablespoons cooking oil

2 tablespoons minced garlic

2 tablespoons minced fresh ginger

2 tablespoons minced green onions, white part only

1 lb. (450g) small Asian eggplant, sliced

2 tablespoons dark soy sauce

2 tablespoons chile bean paste or black-bean sauce

1 tablespoon sugar

1 tablespoon cider vinegar

2 teaspoons peppercorns, roasted and ground

1 cup (250ml) vegetable stock, page 10, or water

1. Heat non-stick wok or skillet until very hot. Add oil and when it is hot add garlic, ginger and green onions and stir-fry 30 seconds. Add eggplant and stir-fry 1-2 minutes longer.

2. Add remaining ingredients and simmer, uncovered, 10-15 minutes until tender. Increase heat and stir until liquid has thickened. Serve sprinkled with green onions.

Makes 4 servings.

GARNISH

2 tablespoons chopped green onions, tops only

Each serving contains:

				Tot.	Sat.		
Cal	Prot	Carb	Fib	Fat	Fat	Chol	Sodium
140	3g	18g	4g	7g	1g	0mg	674mg

HOT TOSSED CABBAGE Ⓥ

Toasted seeds and orange juice give a wonderfully aromatic flavor to this unusual cabbage dish. Serve with rice and curries or with Jamaican Run Down, page 98, or Balaton Hotpot, page 94.

2 tablespoons raisins

1/4 cup (60ml) orange juice

A little grated orange peel

2 tablespoons cider vinegar

3 tablespoons cooking oil

1 teaspoon whole cumin seeds

1 teaspoon black or yellow mustard seeds

1 onion, peeled and sliced

1-1/2 cups (175g) green cabbage, finely shredded

3/4 cup (75g) red cabbage, finely shredded

GARNISH

2 tablespoons flaked almonds, toasted

1. Combine raisins, orange juice, orange peel and vinegar. Set aside.

2. Heat oil in a large non-stick skillet or wok. Sauté the whole spices about 1 minute until they begin to pop. Add onion and cabbage and stir-fry 3-4 minutes.

3. Add raisin mixture and cook 1-2 minutes longer. Serve hot from the pan, garnished with toasted flaked almonds.

Makes 4 servings.

Each serving contains:

Cal	Prot	Carb	Fib	Tot. Fat	Sat. Fat	Chol	Sodium
157	2g	11g	2g	12g	2g	0mg	9mg

ZUCCHINI WITH GARLIC AND OLIVES ⓥ

These flavors are closer to those of Mediterranean dishes than Chinese, but the combination works well as a stir-fry and can be accompanied by simple egg noodles. Start the meal with Red-Pepper Salad, page 38.

2 tablespoons olive oil

2 shallots or 4-6 green onions, minced

2-3 cloves garlic, peeled and sliced

1 lb. (450g) zucchini, trimmed and cut into large dice

16-20 black olives, pitted and chopped

Salt and pepper to taste

4-5 tablespoons vegetable stock, page 10

1 tablespoon dry sherry

1. Heat oil in a non-stick wok or deep skillet. Stir-fry shallots or green onions and garlic for 1 minute.

2. Add zucchini and continue to stir-fry another 2-3 minutes, depending on size of the dice. Add remaining ingredients and bring to a boil. Cook over high heat 1 minute and serve.

Makes 4 servings.

Each serving contains:

Cal	Prot	Carb	Fib	Tot. Fat	Sat. Fat	Chol	Sodium
116	2g	7g	3g	9g	1g	0mg	271mg

MIXED VEGETABLES WITH CASHEWS ⓥ

Carrots can take quite a long time to cook in a wok and they tend to remain much harder than the other vegetables. The solution is to use a potato peeler to cut them into long, thin curls which cook quickly.

2 tablespoons cooking oil

1 piece (1-inch / 2.5cm) fresh ginger, peeled and grated

2 cloves garlic, peeled and chopped

1 onion, peeled and finely sliced

1/2 small bunch celery, finely sliced

6 oz. (175g) green beans

3-1/2 oz. (100g) sugar peas

1 carrot, peeled and cut into strips

Juice of 1 orange

1 tablespoon light soy sauce

2 tablespoons toasted cashew nuts

Freshly ground black pepper

1. Heat oil in a non-stick wok or deep skillet and stir-fry ginger, garlic and onion for 1 minute. Add celery and cook 2 minutes.

2. Add beans and stir-fry 1 minute. Add sugar peas and carrot and stir-fry about 2 minutes longer.

3. Add remaining ingredients. Increase heat and boil 1 minute until the vegetables are cooked as desired.

Makes 4 servings.

Each serving contains:

Cal	Prot	Carb	Fib	Tot. Fat	Sat. Fat	Chol	Sodium
151	3g	16g	4g	9g	1g	0mg	395mg

CHINESE LEAVES WITH LEMON GRASS ⓥ

The inspiration for this recipe comes from Thai cooking and it has a spicy, sweet/sour quality that is quite unusual with greens. Serve it as part of an Eastern medley of dishes with Singapore Noodles, page 147, Okra with Coconut, page 99, and Tofu-Topped Mushrooms, page 122.

2 tablespoons cooking oil

3 pieces of lemon grass, cut into 2-to-3-inch (5-7.5cm) lengths

2 cloves garlic, peeled and sliced

1/2 head Chinese cabbage, sliced

6-8 bok choy leaves, torn into pieces

1/4 cup (60ml) white wine

1 teaspoon light soy sauce

Salt and pepper to taste

1/2 teaspoon sugar

1/4 teaspoon cayenne or chili pepper

1 small bunch of fresh cilantro or coriander, coarsely chopped

1. Heat oil in a non-stick wok or deep skillet and stir-fry lemon grass and garlic for a minute.

2. Add cabbage leaves and stir-fry 2 minutes. Add remaining ingredients except cilantro or coriander and bring to a boil. Cook 1 minute and add cilantro or coriander. Cook 1 minute longer and serve.

Makes 4 servings.

Each serving contains:

Cal	Prot	Carb	Fib	Tot. Fat	Sat. Fat	Chol	Sodium
86	2g	3g	1g	7g	1g	0mg	223mg

SPINACH WITH VEGETABLES AND HAZELNUTS Ⓥ

I live near a wonderful delicatessen which constantly seeks out and offers new ingredients for its customers to try. As a result I have tried sun-dried eggplant and peppers as well as the more-common sun-dried tomatoes. Whichever you can find will work well in this recipe, which is half Italian and half Chinese.

2 oz. (60g) sun-dried tomatoes or mixed sun-dried vegetables

1-1/2 lb. (675g) fresh leaf spinach, stalks removed

2 tablespoons olive oil

1 clove garlic, peeled and crushed

Salt and pepper to taste

Pinch nutmeg

2 tablespoons chopped hazelnuts

1. Cover sun-dried vegetables with boiling water and let stand 10-15 minutes.
2. Rinse spinach thoroughly and dry on paper towels.
3. Drain soaked vegetables, reserving liquid, and slice thinly.
4. Heat olive oil in a non-stick wok or deep skillet and sauté garlic 30 seconds. Add spinach and sliced vegetables and stir-fry 1 minute.
5. Add remaining ingredients and a little of the vegetable-soaking liquid. Bring to a boil and serve at once.

Makes 4 servings.

Each serving contains:

Cal	Prot	Carb	Fib	Tot. Fat	Sat. Fat	Chol	Sodium
158	7g	15g	7g	10g	1g	0mg	498mg

BRAISED RADICCHIO Ⓥ

Radicchio lettuce remains reasonably firm when cooked in sauce and works well in this Chinese braising recipe. You could also try Swiss chard or kale.

Juice and grated peel of 1 orange

2 tablespoons soy sauce

1 tablespoon sherry

1 teaspoon grated fresh ginger

1/4 teaspoon Chinese five-spice powder

1 tablespoon raisins

4 heads radicchio or Belgian endive, cut into quarters

1. Pour orange juice, soy sauce and sherry into a wok or skillet. Add orange peel, fresh ginger, Chinese five-spice powder and raisins.

2. Bring to a boil and cook 1 minute. Add radicchio or endive and cook 2-3 minutes until lettuce is heated through. It should be slightly softened but not limp.

Makes 4 servings.

Each serving contains:

Cal	Prot	Carb	Fib	Tot. Fat	Sat. Fat	Chol	Sodium
31	1g	6g	0g	0g	0g	0mg	660mg

ASPARAGUS AND SUGAR PEAS ⓥ

The lemony flavors of lemon grass, tamarind paste and lemons themselves are widely used in oriental cooking. I have tried matching them with different vegetables. This recipe uses fresh lemons with asparagus and sugar peas to give a clean flavor to a stir-fry dish in the Chinese style. You could replace the lemon with tamarind paste and add a teaspoonful of honey and some chili pepper to give a Thai feel to the dish.

2 tablespoons cooking oil

1 lemon, finely sliced

1 clove garlic, crushed

3/4 lb. (340g) asparagus, halved

6 oz. (175g) sugar peas, trimmed

Juice of 1 lemon

3 tablespoons vegetable stock,
   page 10

1 tablespoon light soy sauce

Salt and pepper to taste

1/2 teaspoon cornstarch,
   mixed with 2 teaspoons
   water (optional)

1. Heat oil in a wok or deep skillet. Carefully add lemon slices—they may spatter when added to hot oil. Stir-fry 1-2 minutes.

2. Remove lemon slices, reserving about half of the thinnest and discarding the rest.

3. Return pan to the heat and add garlic. Stir in vegetables. Stir-fry 2 minutes and add reserved lemon slices and remaining ingredients, except cornstarch mixture.

4. Bring mixture to a boil, cook 2-3 minutes. If desired, stir in cornstarch mixture and boil until liquid has thickened.

Makes 4 servings.

Each serving contains:

Cal	Prot	Carb	Fib	Tot. Fat	Sat. Fat	Chol	Sodium
117	5g	12g	5g	7g	1g	0mg	407mg

DICED HALLOUMI CHEESE WITH PEAS

Serve this colorful mixture with fried noodles or boiled bulgur. Add cheese at the very last minute; be careful not to overcook it.

2 tablespoons cooking oil

1 clove garlic, peeled and crushed

6-8 green onions, chopped

1 red bell pepper, seeded and diced

2 oz. (60g) frozen corn

6 oz. (175g) frozen peas

1 tablespoon sherry

3 tablespoons vegetable stock, page 10

Salt and pepper to taste

Pinch of Chinese five-spice powder

2 tablespoons chopped fresh parsley

1 tablespoon chopped fresh basil

6 oz. (175g) Halloumi cheese, finely diced

1. Heat oil in a wok or deep skillet and stir-fry garlic and green onions 1 minute.
2. Add bell pepper and continue stir-frying another 2 minutes. Add frozen vegetables and mix.
3. Add sherry, stock, salt, pepper and Chinese five-spice powder and increase the heat. Stir-fry 2-3 minutes.
4. Add remaining ingredients and toss for 30 seconds to warm through. Serve at once.

Makes 4 servings.

Each serving contains:

Cal	Prot	Carb	Fib	Tot. Fat	Sat. Fat	Chol	Sodium
242	12g	13g	4g	16g	7g	34mg	268mg

Chapter Eight

PASTA AND NOODLES

Pasta is an essential item for any pantry as it is one of the most useful convenience foods. It does not take up much space yet expands to about three times its volume on cooking. Sauces can easily be made in the time that the pasta takes to cook.

Good Parmesan cheese adds the finishing touch to most pasta dishes, so do buy pieces cut from a whole cheese and grate it yourself just before you are going to use it. Avoid ready-grated Parmesan—at best it will be tired and at worst it will taste like sawdust. Parmesan cheese will keep in a cool, dry place for a long time. If your kitchen is warm, store the cheese in the refrigerator.

Chinese egg noodles and Japanese buckwheat noodles not only give an authentic flavor to oriental dishes, but also add interest to other quick meals. The recipe for Singapore Noodles gives you the opportunity to personalize the recipe by using your choice of optional ingredients.

SPAGHETTINI WITH PEAS AND HERBS

This dish is simple to make and it is truly delicious. It comes from the Veneto area of Northeastern Italy and I first tried it in a little restaurant just off the Grand Canal in Venice. Butter is essential, so don't be tempted to use margarine, cooking oil or even a good olive oil.

1 lb. (450g) fresh or frozen peas
6 tablespoons (75g) softened butter
1/4 cup (60ml) chopped fresh parsley
1/4 cup (60ml) chopped fresh basil
2 tablespoons chopped fresh chives
1 clove garlic, peeled and crushed
3/4 lb. (340g) dried spaghettini
Salt and pepper to taste
Freshly grated Parmesan cheese

1. Steam fresh peas in a steamer, or in a covered saucepan, 5-8 minutes. If you are using frozen peas, cook as directed on the package.
2. Put butter in a bowl and mix in herbs and garlic.
3. Cook spaghettini in salted boiling water as directed on package.
4. Drain spaghettini well and return to the hot pan. Add peas and herb butter and toss together. Serve at once with salt, pepper and Parmesan cheese.

Makes 4 servings.

Each serving contains:

Cal	Prot	Carb	Fib	Tot. Fat	Sat. Fat	Chol	Sodium
392	13g	41g	7g	20g	12g	51mg	489mg

SPAGHETTI WITH ZUCCHINI AND MINT

This unusual combination of flavors comes from Tuscany. Mint and zucchini add interest as well as color to this main dish.

2 large cloves garlic, peeled and
*   quartered*
6 tablespoons extra-virgin olive oil
4-5 sprigs of mint
3/4 lb. (340g) dried spaghetti
4 zucchini, sliced
Salt and pepper to taste
Freshly grated Parmesan cheese

1. Put garlic and 4 tablespoons oil in a small bowl. Strip leaves from mint sprigs and add to the bowl. Set aside.

2. Cook spaghetti in salted boiling water 8-10 minutes or as directed on package. Drain.

3. While pasta is cooking, sauté zucchini in remaining oil 8-10 minutes until golden.

4. Remove garlic from oil and discard. Pour oil and mint over pasta and add zucchini. Toss well and serve with Parmesan cheese and black pepper.

Makes 4 servings.

Each serving contains:

Cal	Prot	Carb	Fib	Tot. Fat	Sat. Fat	Chol	Sodium
346	8g	28g	2g	23g	4g	5mg	187mg

SPAGHETTI WITH ASPARAGUS

This delicately flavored dish is most delicious when the asparagus season is at its best in May and June. However, if you prefer not to use fresh asparagus in this way, frozen asparagus is quite good.

3/4 lb. (340g) fresh or frozen asparagus

1/2 cup (125ml) whipping cream

1/4 cup (60ml) vegetable stock, page 10

Salt and pepper to taste

3/4 lb. (340g) dried spaghetti

1 tablespoon olive oil

1/4 cup freshly grated Parmesan cheese

1. Steam asparagus until tender. Cut off the tips and set aside.

2. In a food processor or blender purée stems with a little cream.

3. Transfer to a saucepan. Add remaining cream and stock and bring to a boil. Cook over medium heat to thicken sauce. Season with salt and pepper.

4. Meanwhile, cook spaghetti in salted boiling water 8-10 minutes or as directed on package. Drain and toss in olive oil.

5. Pour asparagus sauce over pasta and toss together. Garnish with asparagus tips and Parmesan cheese.

Makes 4 servings.

Each serving contains:

Cal	Prot	Carb	Fib	Tot. Fat	Sat. Fat	Chol	Sodium
306	10g	30g	3g	17g	9g	46mg	199mg

SPAGHETTI WITH SUNFLOWER SEEDS

This sauce may seem a bit too dry when you are making it, but it's fine once it is mixed with the pasta. So avoid the temptation to add too much oil or the flavors will be diluted. Good herbs to use are sage, mint and thyme.

3/4 lb. (340g) dried spaghetti
2 oz. (60g) sunflower seeds
1-1/2 oz. (45g) sun-dried-tomato
  paste
2 cloves garlic, peeled and crushed
Freshly ground black pepper
Olive oil
1/3 cup (80ml) fresh herbs,
  chopped or shredded
Freshly grated Parmesan cheese

1. Cook spaghetti in salted boiling water 8-10 minutes or as directed on package.
2. In a dry skillet, toast sunflower seeds until golden.
3. Allow pan to cool slightly. Stir in tomato paste, garlic, pepper and a little olive oil, depending on how much there is in the paste. Stir over medium heat for about 1 minute.
4. Drain cooked spaghetti and place in a heated serving bowl. Stir in sauce and herbs.
5. Serve with more olive oil and Parmesan cheese.

Makes 4 servings.

Each serving contains:

Cal	Prot	Carb	Fib	Tot. Fat	Sat. Fat	Chol	Sodium
289	11g	33g	3g	13g	3g	5mg	341mg

Opposite: California Lima Beans, page 90, served with stir-fried vegetables and broccoli tossed with slivered almonds

TAGLIATELLE WITH TOASTED SEEDS

This simple dish from the hills above Lake Garda has a wonderful flavor and an unusual texture. You can make it with cream or extra-virgin olive oil, whichever you prefer.

3/4 lb. (340g) dried tagliatelle

Salt

2 tablespoons pumpkin seeds

2 tablespoons sunflower seeds

2 tablespoons pine nuts

6 tablespoons (75ml) whipping cream or extra-virgin olive oil

Freshly ground black pepper

Freshly grated Parmesan cheese

1. Cook pasta in salted boiling water 6-7 minutes or as directed on package.

2. In a dry skillet, toast seeds and pine nuts until browned.

3. Drain pasta well and toss with seeds, nuts and cream or olive oil. Serve with black pepper and Parmesan cheese.

Makes 4 servings.

Each serving contains:

Cal	Prot	Carb	Fib	Tot. Fat	Sat. Fat	Chol	Sodium
296	10g	28g	2g	17g	8g	35mg	193mg

Opposite: Mixed Vegetables with Cashews, page 126, and Singapore Noodles, page 147

RIGATONI WITH PEANUT-BUTTER SAUCE

If you are a peanut-butter fan you will love this sauce for chunky tubular rigatoni. Even if you are not fond of peanut butter you should give this unusual sauce a try.

3/4 lb. (340g) dried rigatoni
Salt
2 onions, peeled and minced
2 cloves garlic, peeled and crushed
1 teaspoon grated lemon rind
2 teaspoons olive oil
1/4 cup smooth peanut butter
1 cup (250ml) milk
Freshly ground black pepper
1/4 cup (60ml) chopped fresh mixed herbs such as parsley, basil or tarragon

1. Cook pasta in salted boiling water 8-10 minutes or as directed on package.

2. In a large non-stick pan, sauté onion, garlic and lemon rind in olive oil.

3. Gradually stir in peanut butter and milk and bring to a boil, adding a little more milk if sauce gets too thick.

4. Drain rigatoni; add to sauce. Toss together and season with pepper. Serve sprinkled with chopped fresh herbs.

Makes 4 servings.

Each serving contains:

Cal	Prot	Carb	Fib	Tot. Fat	Sat. Fat	Chol	Sodium
289	11g	36g	3g	12g	3g	5mg	178mg

UMBRIAN CHICKPEAS AND PASTA ⓥ

Chickpeas, or garbanzos, are a popular ingredient in the pasta dishes of Central Italy. For a change include white kidney beans, pink beans or whole lentils.

3/4 lb. (340g) dried pasta such as fusilli, bows or macaroni elbows

3 tablespoons extra-virgin olive oil

3 stalks (1-1/2 cups) chopped celery

1 can (8 oz. / 225g) chickpeas or garbanzos

1/4 cup (60ml) dry white wine

3 tomatoes, peeled, seeded and chopped

Salt and pepper to taste

1/4 cup (60ml) chopped fresh chives

1 tablespoon chopped fresh parsley

1/4 cup (60ml) freshly grated Parmesan cheese

1. Cook pasta in salted boiling water as directed on package. Drain well.

2. Heat oil in a saucepan and sauté celery 4-5 minutes.

3. Add chickpeas or garbanzos, wine and tomatoes and bring to a boil. Reduce heat and simmer 4-5 minutes longer.

4. Add pasta, salt, pepper, chives and parsley. Toss all together and serve at once, sprinkled with Parmesan cheese.

Makes 4 servings.

Each serving contains:

Cal	Prot	Carb	Fib	Tot. Fat	Sat. Fat	Chol	Sodium
331	10g	40g	6g	14g	3g	5mg	355mg

THREE-MUSHROOM PASTA IN CREAM SAUCE

Everyone loves this creamy pasta dish, which I serve straight from the pan. If you cannot find dried mushrooms or oyster or brown mushrooms use 1 pound (450g) button mushrooms.

4 or 5 dried mushrooms

2 tablespoons (25g) pine nuts or flaked almonds

8 oz. (225g) plain dried noodles

1/4 cup (50g) butter

1/2 lb. (225g) button mushrooms, sliced

1/4 lb. (115g) oyster or brown mushrooms, sliced

1/2 cup (125ml) whipping cream

Pinch of ground nutmeg

Freshly ground black pepper

1. Pour boiling water over dried mushrooms and soak for 10 minutes.

2. In a hot dry skillet, toast pine nuts or almonds. Cook noodles in salted boiling water 8-10 minutes or as directed on package. Drain and keep warm.

3. Drain mushrooms and cut off stems. Slice tops thinly. Melt butter in a large skillet and sauté all mushrooms 3-4 minutes until they soften.

4. Add cream, nutmeg and pepper and bring to a boil. Add pasta and toss together. Sprinkle with toasted pine nuts or almonds and serve.

Makes 4 servings.

Each serving contains:

Cal	Prot	Carb	Fib	Tot. Fat	Sat. Fat	Chol	Sodium
356	7g	25g	3g	27g	15g	72mg	133mg

CARROT-AND-TARRAGON CARBONARA SAUCE

The sauce should be very creamy with the eggs hardly set. Too often Carbonara sauces are grainy because the eggs are overcooked. If you work quickly the eggs can be tossed with the pasta after it has been taken off the heat—there should be sufficient heat in it to cook the eggs to the right consistency.

3/4 lb. (340g) dried fettuccine

2 carrots, peeled and diced

1 tablespoon minced shallots or onion

1 tablespoon olive oil or butter

3 eggs, beaten

6 tablespoons (50g) freshly grated Parmesan cheese

2 tablespoons chopped fresh tarragon

Salt and pepper to taste

Freshly grated Parmesan, to serve

1. Cook fettuccine in salted boiling water 7-8 minutes or as directed on package.
2. Sauté carrots and onion in oil or butter 6-7 minutes.
3. Mix eggs, cheese, tarragon, salt and pepper.
4. Drain pasta and toss with hot carrots and egg mixture.
5. Serve with more Parmesan cheese and black pepper.

Makes 4 servings.

Each serving contains:

Cal	Prot	Carb	Fib	Tot. Fat	Sat. Fat	Chol	Sodium
298	16g	30g	2g	13g	5g	172mg	419mg

PASTA WITH LEEK-AND-GARLIC SAUCE

You can use any kind of garlic-flavored cheese for this well-flavored quickie. Boursin, Bressot or garlic roulade all work well. Serve with any kind of chunky pasta such as penne, rigatoni or fusilli.

3/4 lb. (340g) dried pasta

3-4 leeks trimmed and thickly sliced

6 oz. (175g) Boursin cheese

3 tablespoons whipping cream

Freshly ground black pepper

2 tablespoons chopped fresh parsley

1. Cook pasta in salted boiling water as directed on package. Drain well.

2. Meanwhile, steam leeks 5-8 minutes until softened but still tender-crisp.

3. In a small saucepan, heat cheese and cream. Stir until cheese has melted; bring to a boil and remove from heat.

4. Stir in leeks, black pepper and parsley.

5. Place pasta in a warm serving bowl and top with sauce.

Makes 4 servings.

Each serving contains:

Cal	Prot	Carb	Fib	Tot. Fat	Sat. Fat	Chol	Sodium
383	9g	43g	4g	20g	12g	62mg	157mg

PASTA BOWS WITH GOAT-CHEESE SAUCE

Soft goat cheese melts easily to make an instant creamy, slightly tangy sauce. Seeds are used not only to add extra dimension to the flavor, but also to give an unusual crunchy texture. Poppy seeds are very popular in Hungary, where they are used in both sweet and savory dishes.

3/4 lb. (340g) pasta bows

Salt

1 tablespoon poppy seeds or sesame seeds

1 onion, peeled and minced

2 tablespoons cooking oil

1/4 cup (60ml) white wine

2 tablespoons vegetable stock, page 10

6 oz. (175g) fresh goat cheese such as Perroche or Pyramid, cut into small chunks

Freshly ground black pepper

Freshly grated hard goat cheese or Pecorino cheese

1. Cook pasta in salted boiling water 7-8 minutes or as directed on package. Drain.

2. In a dry skillet, toast poppy seeds or sesame seeds over medium heat 1 minute or so. Set aside.

3. Sauté onion in oil 2-3 minutes until softened; do not brown.

4. Add wine and stock to onion and stir in cheese. When cheese is melted, stir in black pepper and toasted seeds. Heat through.

5. Toss pasta with sauce. Serve with freshly ground black pepper and grated hard goat cheese or Pecorino cheese.

Makes 4 servings.

Each serving contains:

Cal	Prot	Carb	Fib	Tot. Fat	Sat. Fat	Chol	Sodium
433	20g	28g	2g	25g	13g	50mg	333mg

FUSILLI WITH WILD MUSHROOMS

This pasta dish comes from Verona and is usually served only when fresh *porcini* (cep) mushrooms are in season. However, I make it all year round with dried mushrooms of one kind or another. The flavor varies depending on the type used but it is always good.

1/2 oz. (15g) dried porcini or ceps, or other dried mushrooms

3/4 lb. (340g) dried fusilli

1 small onion, peeled and chopped

2 cloves garlic, peeled and crushed

2 tablespoons olive oil

1 small carrot, peeled and minced

1 stalk celery, minced

1 can (8-oz. / 225g) cannellini beans, drained

1 teaspoon tomato purée

2 tablespoons white wine

Salt and pepper to taste

4 fresh sage leaves, chopped

Freshly grated Parmesan cheese

1. Cover mushrooms with boiling water. Soak 20 minutes.

2. Cook pasta in salted boiling water 7-8 minutes or as directed on package.

3. Sauté onion and garlic in oil 3-4 minutes until lightly browned. Add carrot and celery and cook 3-4 minutes.

4. Add cannellini beans, tomato purée, wine, mushrooms and soaking liquid. Bring to a boil and simmer 10 minutes until vegetables are cooked. Season with salt and pepper.

5. Drain pasta and toss with sage and cooked vegetables. Serve with Parmesan cheese.

Makes 4 servings.

Each serving contains:

Cal	Prot	Carb	Fib	Tot. Fat	Sat. Fat	Chol	Sodium
288	11g	38g	5g	10g	2g	5mg	324mg

RAVIOLI-AND-EGGPLANT SAUCERS

Here's a great way to pep up canned or frozen ravioli. It makes a good lunch or supper dish. Individual servings can be frozen before cooking, then thawed and used later.

1 large eggplant, sliced

2 tablespoons cooking oil

1 can (14-oz. / 400g) ravioli in tomato sauce or 1 (18-oz.) package frozen, thawed

1 cup (250ml) sour cream or plain yogurt

2/3 cup (75g) fresh breadcrumbs

3/4 cup (75g) grated Cheddar cheese

1. Preheat broiler. Grease four heatproof saucers or gratin dishes.

2. Brush eggplant slices on both sides with oil and broil 2-3 minutes a side until lightly browned and tender.

3. Meanwhile, heat ravioli in a saucepan.

4. Arrange eggplant slices on prepared saucers or dishes. Top with ravioli and then with sour cream or yogurt. Combine breadcrumbs and cheese and sprinkle on top. Broil 5-6 minutes.

Makes 4 servings.

Each serving contains:

Cal	Prot	Carb	Fib	Tot. Fat	Sat. Fat	Chol	Sodium
459	15g	30g	4g	32g	15g	111mg	816mg

FRIED EGG NOODLES

This is my simplified version of an authentic Indonesian noodle dish. It can be served with any of the recipes in the Wok Cookery chapter.

2 tablespoons cooking oil

2 eggs, beaten

8 oz. (225g) Chinese egg noodles

1 clove garlic, peeled and crushed

2 tablespoons minced ginger

1 onion, peeled and minced

2 stalks celery, finely sliced

1 tablespoon soy sauce

2 tablespoons sherry

6-8 green onions, sliced lengthwise

1. Heat 1 tablespoon oil in skillet and pour in beaten eggs. Allow eggs to spread out to make a large flat omelet. When it is cooked through, remove and cut into strips. Keep warm.

2. Cook noodles in salted boiling water for 5 minutes or as directed on package. Drain and set aside.

3. Meanwhile, sauté garlic, ginger, onion and celery in remaining oil 5-8 minutes, stirring constantly, until tender.

4. Add soy sauce, sherry and noodles. Heat through, stirring well to distribute sauce through the noodles.

5. Serve garnished with slices of green onion and omelet strips.

Makes 4 servings.

Each serving contains:

Cal	Prot	Carb	Fib	Tot. Fat	Sat. Fat	Chol	Sodium
203	7g	20g	2g	10g	2g	125mg	387mg

SINGAPORE NOODLES Ⓥ

Every Chinese restaurant I have been to seems to have its own recipe for Singapore Noodles but the flavoring they all have in common is red chile peppers.

The basic recipe makes an excellent partner to most stir-fry dishes and dishes such as Chickpeas with Spinach, page 93, or Tagine of Okra and Tomatoes, page 97. Alternatively you can add any or all of the optional extras to make an even more interesting dish.

1/2 lb. (225g) Chinese egg noodles

1 tablespoon cooking oil

1/2 lb. (225g) fresh bean sprouts

1 teaspoon soy sauce

2-3 fresh red chile peppers, seeded and finely sliced

OPTIONAL EXTRAS

1/2 teaspoon sesame oil

2 tablespoons cooked peas

2 tablespoons cooked corn

2 tablespoons diced bamboo shoots

2 oz. (60g) blanched sugar peas

4-6 green onions, trimmed and sliced in half lengthwise

1. Cook noodles in salted boiling water as directed on package. Drain well.

2. Heat oil in a large pan and toss in bean sprouts. Add noodles, soy sauce and optional extras, if using, and toss together. Heat through, add chile peppers and serve at once.

Makes 4 servings.

Each serving contains:

Cal	Prot	Carb	Fib	Tot. Fat	Sat. Fat	Chol	Sodium
137	5g	21g	2g	4g	1g	19mg	119mg

JAPANESE NOODLES WITH TAMARI SAUCE Ⓥ

Japanese buckwheat noodles can be used in much the same way as Chinese egg noodles. They have a good flavor of their own and need punchy flavors to go with them. *Tamari* is Japanese soy sauce.

10 oz. (280g) Japanese buckwheat noodles

2 tablespoons cooking oil

2 tablespoons grated fresh ginger

2 cloves garlic, peeled and crushed

2-3 green onions, minced

3 tablespoons tamari sauce

Freshly ground black pepper

1. Cook noodles as directed on package. Drain.

2. Heat cooking oil in a wok or deep skillet and add ginger, garlic and green onions. Stir-fry 2 minutes.

3. Add drained noodles and stir-fry another minute or so. Add tamari sauce and black pepper and bring to a boil. Serve at once.

Makes 4 servings.

Each serving contains:

Cal	Prot	Carb	Fib	Tot. Fat	Sat. Fat	Chol	Sodium
141	5g	17g	1g	7g	1g	0mg	651mg

Chapter Nine

RICE AND GRAINS

Rice and grains, such as bulgur and couscous, join noodles and pasta as convenience foods par excellence. All are easy to cook.

Cooking times for the rice recipes are based on long-grain white rice. If you prefer to use brown rice you need to add a little more water and increase cooking time by 5-10 minutes depending upon the type of rice. Follow package instructions.

The risottos are best made with Italian Arborio or risotto rice. These give a creamier, more authentic result than American or basmati rice, which remain a little too separate.

The recipes in this chapter are taken from all around the world— Empedrado Madrileño from Spain, Polenta Rustica from Italy, Couscous-and-Vegetable Ragout from Morocco and Spicy Corn Pilaf from the U.S. Most of them can be eaten alone with a simple mixed salad or with grilled vegetables or fruits.

TURKISH RICE Ⓥ

This wonderfully aromatic rice dish is good enough to eat on its own. It is also good served with Lentil Burgers, page 116. Pistachios give an authentic flavor to the dish.

3 tablespoons olive oil

1 small onion, peeled and minced

1 cup (225g) long-grain rice

1 teaspoon salt

Freshly ground black pepper

1 tomato, peeled, seeded and minced

2 tablespoons pine nuts

1 tablespoon pistachios, roughly chopped (optional)

2 tablespoons (25g) raisins

1 tablespoon chopped fresh parsley

1/2 tablespoon chopped fresh sage

1/2 tablespoon chopped fresh mint

1/4 teaspoon ground mixed spice

2 cups (500ml) vegetable stock, page 10

1. In a large pan, heat 2 tablespoons oil. Add onion and rice and sauté 2 minutes, stirring constantly. Add remaining ingredients except stock, and continue cooking and stirring another 3 minutes.

2. Pour in stock and bring to a boil. Cover and cook over low heat 12-15 minutes, until rice is tender and liquid absorbed.

3. Remove pan from heat. Let stand 5 minutes. Add remaining oil and serve.

Makes 4 servings.

Each serving contains:

Cal	Prot	Carb	Fib	Tot. Fat	Sat. Fat	Chol	Sodium
221	4g	22g	3g	14g	2g	0mg	546mg

MEXICAN RICE

This spicy rice dish is so good I often serve it as an entrée, along with a green salad with avocados. It also makes a good accompaniment to simple kebabs or grilled burgers.

1 tablespoon (15g) butter

1 cup (225g) long-grain rice

1 can (14-oz. / 400g) tomatoes

1 cup (250ml) vegetable stock, page 10

Salt and pepper to taste

1/2-1 teaspoon ground chili powder

1 red bell pepper, sliced into rings, seeds removed

1 green bell pepper, sliced into rings, seeds removed

1 onion, peeled and sliced

1. Melt butter in a non-stick pan. Sauté rice and add tomatoes and their juice, stock, salt, pepper and chili powder to taste. Bring to a boil and stir.

2. Lay peppers and onions on top. Cover and simmer 20 minutes until liquid is absorbed and rice is tender.

Makes 4 servings.

Each serving contains:

Cal	Prot	Carb	Fib	Tot. Fat	Sat. Fat	Chol	Sodium
126	3g	22g	3g	4g	2g	8mg	271mg

EGYPTIAN RICE

Rice is surprisingly popular in Egypt but the spicing is quite different from that used in other parts of the Eastern Mediterranean. This is another rice recipe that is substantial enough to eat as a main course, accompanied, perhaps, by a simple tossed green salad. However, there is no reason why you should not serve it with one of the simpler stir-fries in Chapter 7.

1 onion, peeled and minced

2 tablespoons (25g) butter

1 clove garlic, peeled and chopped

1 tablespoon chopped fresh cilantro or coriander

1 tablespoon chopped fresh basil

1/4 teaspoon turmeric

1/4 teaspoon dried thyme

1/4 teaspoon cayenne pepper

Salt and pepper to taste

1/4 cup (50g) chopped raisins

3 tablespoons (50g) chopped almonds

1 cup (225g) long-grain rice

2 cups (500ml) water

2 oz. (50g) vermicelli or spaghetti

1 tablespoon olive oil

1. Sauté onion in butter in a heavy-based pan until it turns golden brown.

2. Add remaining ingredients except vermicelli or spaghetti and olive oil. Bring to a boil. Stir and cover.

3. Reduce heat and simmer 20 minutes until liquid is absorbed and rice is tender.

4. Break vermicelli or spaghetti into short lengths and cook in salted boiling water 6-8 minutes until tender. Drain well. Heat oil in a small pan and stir-fry pasta until golden.

6. Fluff rice with a fork and stir in pasta.

Makes 4 servings.

Each serving contains:

Cal	Prot	Carb	Fib	Tot. Fat	Sat. Fat	Chol	Sodium
228	4g	26g	2g	13g	4g	16mg	134mg

EGG-AND-CARROT PILAF

I serve this pilaf with Okra with Coconut, page 99. There is something seductive about the combination of cardamom, raisin and coconut. A green salad makes a good accompaniment.

4 onions, peeled

4 tablespoons cooking oil

1 cup (225g) long-grain rice

2 carrots, peeled and grated

2 tablespoons raisins

1-1/2 cups (375ml) vegetable stock, page 10

1 tablespoon minced parsley

1 tablespoon minced mint

Salt and pepper to taste

6 eggs

3-4 cardamom pods or 1/4 teaspoon ground cardamom

1. Mince two onions; slice the others into rings and set aside.

2. Sauté minced onions in 2 tablespoons oil. Add rice and cook another 1-2 minutes, stirring constantly.

3. Add carrots, raisins, stock, parsley, mint, salt and pepper. Bring to a boil, cover and simmer 15-20 minutes. Remove from heat; stir and cover. Set aside 15 minutes.

4. Cook eggs in simmering water 12-14 minutes. Rinse in cold water, drain, peel and slice.

5. Remove seeds from cardamom pods, discard pods. Sauté seeds in remaining oil 30 seconds. Add sliced onions and cook until crisp and brown.

6. Fluff rice; serve topped with sliced eggs and onion rings.

Makes 4 servings.

Each serving contains:

Cal	Prot	Carb	Fib	Tot. Fat	Sat. Fat	Chol	Sodium
365	13g	31g	5g	22g	4g	319mg	185mg

SPANISH RICE WITH PEPPERS ⓥ

This simple rice dish is typical of the resourcefulness of regional cooking in the poorer areas of Spain, and it works beautifully. Traditionally it is prepared in large quantities with whole peppers. I have cut the peppers into strips for faster cooking.

1/2 small onion, peeled and chopped

3 tablespoons olive oil

1 cup (225g) long-grain rice

2 small green bell peppers, seeded and cut into strips

1 red bell pepper, seeded and cut into strips

Salt and white pepper to taste

A few strands of saffron (optional)

2 cups (500ml) water

1. Sauté onion in oil until golden and softened.
2. Stir in rice, mixing well. Add bell peppers, salt, pepper and saffron, if using.
3. Pour in water and bring to a boil. Stir, then cover and simmer over low heat 15-20 minutes until rice is tender and liquid is absorbed.

Makes 4 servings.

Each serving contains:

Cal	Prot	Carb	Fib	Tot. Fat	Sat. Fat	Chol	Sodium
159	2g	15g	2g	11g	1g	0mg	74mg

RICE WITH PUMPKIN AND RAISINS ⓥ

This easy Spanish recipe comes from the island of Ibiza. It is quite sweet and goes well with Banana Kebabs, page 110. Use Italian risotto rice, which is more like Spanish rice than American, Patna or basmati varieties. The end result should be drier than a risotto but softer and stickier than a pilau or pilaf.

1 tablespoon olive oil

1 clove garlic, peeled and minced

1/2 lb. (175g) fresh pumpkin or Hubbard squash, diced

1 tablespoon raisins

Salt and pepper to taste

2 cups (500ml) vegetable stock, page 10

10 oz. (280g) risotto rice

Pinch of ground cinnamon

Pinch of sugar

1. Heat oil in a pan and sauté garlic until golden.

2. Add pumpkin or squash, raisins, salt and pepper. Stir and add stock.

3. Bring to a boil and simmer 2-3 minutes. Add rice, cinnamon and sugar and return to boil. Stir and cover. Reduce heat and simmer 12-15 minutes until rice is tender and liquid is absorbed.

4. Let stand covered 3-4 minutes before serving.

Makes 4 servings.

Each serving contains:

Cal	Prot	Carb	Fib	Tot. Fat	Sat. Fat	Chol	Sodium
143	3g	25g	3g	4g	1g	0mg	78mg

EMPEDRADO MADRILEÑO Ⓥ

This dish gets its name from the old method of dry-stone building used for Spanish houses. Small pebbles or gravel were pushed into the cracks between the stones. It is said that the red beans resemble stones while the rice looks like the gravel in between.

1 can (14-oz. / 400g) red kidney beans, drained

3 oz. (85g) basmati rice

2 onions, peeled and chopped

1 clove garlic, peeled and chopped

1 bay leaf

Pinch of salt

3/4 cup (185ml) water

1 tablespoon paprika

2 tablespoons olive oil

1. Place beans and rice in a saucepan; stir in half the onion, the garlic, bay leaf and salt.

2. Pour in water and bring to a boil. Stir once and cover. Reduce heat and simmer 12-15 minutes until rice is tender and water has been absorbed.

3. Meanwhile, sauté remaining onion with paprika in oil 4 minutes, until lightly browned.

4. Stir fried onion into beans and rice and cook 5 minutes. Remove bay leaf and serve.

Makes 4 servings.

Each serving contains:

Cal	Prot	Carb	Fib	Tot. Fat	Sat. Fat	Chol	Sodium
279	10g	44g	11g	8g	1g	0mg	72mg

SPICY CORN PILAF Ⓥ

A friend of mine combined two of her favorite foods, Tabasco® sauce and corn, to create this piquant rice. It goes very well with kebabs.

1 onion, peeled and chopped

2 tablespoons cooking oil

1 cup (225g) basmati rice

3 oz. (85g) corn

1/2 small red bell pepper, seeded and finely chopped

1/2 teaspoon ground cinnamon

1 tablespoon chopped fresh mixed herbs

5-6 drops of Tabasco sauce or 1/2-1 teaspoon chili powder

Salt and pepper to taste

1-1/2 cups (375ml) vegetable stock, page 10, or water

1. Sauté onion in oil until lightly browned. Add rice and stir.

2. Add remaining ingredients and bring to a boil. Stir well and reduce heat.

3. Cover and simmer for 12-15 minutes until all the liquid has been absorbed and rice is tender. Serve.

Makes 4 servings.

Each serving contains:

Cal	Prot	Carb	Fib	Tot. Fat	Sat. Fat	Chol	Sodium
337	7g	63g	5g	8g	1g	0mg	92mg

VENETIAN RISOTTO

Green peas and fennel are both popular in the Veneto region of north-eastern Italy. Here they work together to make an excellent risotto.

2 tablespoons olive oil

2 tablespoons (25g) butter

2 small red onions, peeled and minced

1 clove garlic, peeled and crushed

1 small bulb of fennel, trimmed and minced

2 tablespoons chopped fresh parsley

1 cup (225g) risotto rice

3 oz. (85g) frozen peas

1/2 cup (125ml) dry white wine

Salt and pepper to taste

2-1/4 cups (560ml) vegetable stock, page 10

Butter

Freshly grated Parmesan cheese

1. Heat olive oil and butter in a saucepan and cook onions, garlic and fennel 3-4 minutes until they begin to brown.

2. Add parsley, rice, peas, wine, salt and pepper and bring to a boil. Stirring occasionally, cook, uncovered, 10 minutes until most of the liquid has been absorbed.

3. Add half the stock and return to a boil. Continue cooking and stirring occasionally. When liquid has been absorbed, add remaining stock.

4. Cook until liquid is absorbed, stirring occasionally. The risotto should be slightly creamy. Total cooking time from adding rice will be about 25-30 minutes. Serve with a pat of butter and freshly grated Parmesan cheese.

Makes 4 servings.

Each serving contains:

Cal	Prot	Carb	Fib	Tot. Fat	Sat. Fat	Chol	Sodium
383	9g	39g	10g	21g	10g	36mg	391mg

CARIBBEAN BANANA RISOTTO Ⓥ

The African influence is evident in this delicious risotto. It is very good served sprinkled with toasted pine nuts.

4-6 green onions, chopped

1-inch (2.5cm) piece of fresh ginger, peeled and grated

2 tablespoons cooking oil

A few drops roasted sesame oil

1/4 teaspoon ground allspice

1 fresh green chile pepper, seeded and finely sliced

1 cup (225g) risotto rice

2-1/4 cups (560 ml) vegetable stock, page 10

Salt and pepper to taste

1 large banana

1. Gently sauté green onions and ginger in cooking oil and sesame oil for 2-3 minutes.

2. Add allspice, chile and rice. Stir well and add half the stock. Bring to a boil and cook, uncovered, 10 minutes, stirring occasionally. Do not allow mixture to dry out.

3. Add remaining stock, salt and pepper and return to a boil. Continue to cook 10 minutes, stirring occasionally.

4. Peel and dice banana, stir into rice and continue cooking 5 minutes until rice is tender, liquid has been absorbed and risotto is creamy.

Makes 4 servings.

Each serving contains:

Cal	Prot	Carb	Fib	Tot. Fat	Sat. Fat	Chol	Sodium
171	3g	24g	3g	8g	1g	0mg	82mg

BULGUR-AND-NUT PILAF ⓥ

Make sure you buy quick-cooking bulgur and not cracked wheat, which takes longer to cook. Serve with a tossed fruit salad.

1 small onion, peeled and chopped

2 tablespoons cooking oil

1 small green bell pepper, seeded and chopped

4 oz. (125g) canned or cooked red kidney beans

1/4 cup (50g) cashews, toasted

6 oz. (175g) bulgur

Salt and pepper to taste

1-1/2 cups (375ml) vegetable stock, page 10

1. Sauté onion in oil 2-3 minutes. Add bell pepper and cook for another minute or two.
2. Add remaining ingredients, bring to a boil, stir and cover.
3. Reduce heat and simmer 12-15 minutes until bulgur is cooked and liquid has been absorbed.
4. Fluff up with a fork and serve.

Makes 4 servings.

Each serving contains:

Cal	Prot	Carb	Fib	Tot. Fat	Sat. Fat	Chol	Sodium
288	8g	42g	11g	11g	2g	0mg	147mg

BULGUR WITH FRESH HERBS Ⓥ

This is really a hot version of tabbouleh, though the ratio of bulgur to parsley is higher. It is delicious eaten on its own or it can be served with kebabs.

4-6 green onions, trimmed and chopped

2 tablespoons cooking oil

2 tomatoes, peeled, seeded and chopped

8 oz. (225g) bulgur

Salt and pepper to taste

2 cups (500ml) vegetable stock, page 10

6 tablespoons chopped fresh parsley

1 tablespoon chopped fresh mint

1. Gently sauté green onions in oil for 2-3 minutes.
2. Stir in tomatoes, bulgur, salt, pepper and stock.
3. Bring to a boil, stir and cover. Reduce heat and cook 12-15 minutes until bulgur is cooked and liquid has been absorbed. Stir in herbs.
4. Fluff up with a fork and serve.

Makes 4 servings.

Each serving contains:

Cal	Prot	Carb	Fib	Tot. Fat	Sat. Fat	Chol	Sodium
215	6g	35g	9g	8g	1g	0mg	91mg

COUSCOUS AND VEGETABLE RAGOUT

Couscous is the staple food of North Africa. It looks a little like bulgur but is actually tiny balls of semolina. *Harissa* is a fiery, chile-based sauce from Tunisia.

1 cup (225g) couscous

1 tablespoon (15g) butter

Pinch of ground cinnamon

2 cups (500ml) water

4 carrots, peeled and sliced

1 can (4 oz. / 125g) chickpeas or garbanzos

8 small boiling onions

1 lb. (450g) green beans, broken

1 green or red bell pepper, seeded and cut into small pieces

4 zucchini, trimmed and cut into 1/2-inch (1cm) slices

A few fresh cilantro or coriander leaves

1 tablespoon tomato purée

1 teaspoon paprika

1 teaspoon harissa or chili sauce, or 1/2 teaspoon cayenne pepper

Salt to taste

1. Cook as directed on package. Add butter and cinnamon. Fluff up with fork before serving.

2. To make ragout: Bring water to a boil, then add carrots, chickpeas or garbanzos and onions. Cook 10 minutes. Add beans, pepper and zucchini. Cover and cook 5 minutes until vegetables are tender.

3. Stir in remaining ingredients and serve with couscous.

Makes 4 servings.

Each serving contains:

Cal	Prot	Carb	Fib	Tot. Fat	Sat. Fat	Chol	Sodium
249	9g	48g	12g	4g	2g	8mg	233mg

TAGINE OF TOMATO AND EGG

In North Africa eggs are rarely used in restaurant dishes, but they are used in the home. Hard-cooked eggs with cumin are sold as street snacks. This recipe comes from a friend in Algeria. It's usually served with couscous but you could use bulgur.

6 eggs

1 clove garlic

1 tablespoon olive oil

1 lb. (450g) tomatoes, peeled, seeded and chopped

3 shallots or 1/2 small onion, peeled and minced

Salt and pepper to taste

1/4 teaspoon ground cumin

Cooked couscous, bulgur or savory rice

1. Cook 2 eggs in simmering water 10-12 minutes. Drain, cover with cold water. When cooled, peel and roughly chop.

2. Meanwhile, rub a small heavy-based pan with clove of garlic.

3. Add oil, tomatoes and shallots or onion and cook 15 minutes, stirring occasionally, until thick and mushy.

4. Beat remaining eggs; add to tomato mixture with salt, pepper and cumin. Cook and stir 2-3 minutes until almost set.

5. Add chopped eggs and cook a minute longer; mixture should not be too firm. Serve at once with couscous, bulgur or rice.

Makes 4 servings.

Each serving contains:

Cal	Prot	Carb	Fib	Tot. Fat	Sat. Fat	Chol	Sodium
372	17g	49g	4g	11g	3g	319mg	182mg

POLENTA RUSTICA

It is well worth looking for fast-cooking polenta or cornmeal because it really is ready in minutes. There is no need to stand over it stirring as you have to when using ordinary cornmeal. I first enjoyed polenta in the Val d'Aorta in northwestern Italy, where it is the staple food flavored with the local Fontina cheese. Taleggio cheese is used elsewhere in Italy. If you cannot find these cheeses, substitute Brie. Serve with an endive-and-fennel salad on the side.

1 cup (225g) fast-cooking polenta or cornmeal

2 oz. (50g) Gorgonzola cheese, diced

3 oz. (75g) Fontina, Taleggio or Brie cheese with rind removed, diced

1/4 cup (50g) butter

Salt and pepper to taste

1. Prepare polenta as directed on package, but don't make it too thick.

2. Stir in both cheeses. As soon as cheese has melted and blended with polenta, stir in butter. Add salt and pepper to taste.

Makes 4 servings.

Each serving contains:

Cal	Prot	Carb	Fib	Tot. Fat	Sat. Fat	Chol	Sodium
430	14g	39g	2g	24g	14g	68mg	611mg

INDEX

Ⓥ denotes recipes suitable for vegans.

Quick After-Work Recipe Contest
Fisher Books
4239 W. Ina Road, #101
Tucson, AZ 85741

Enter the Quick After-Work Recipe Contest
Win more than $1,000 in cash and prizes!

The Quick After-Work Recipe Contest runs through August 31, 1996. Prizes will be announced by September 30, 1996. Entries are to be postmarked by August 31, 1996. All entries must be original recipes created by the contestant for the Quick After-Work Recipe Contest. Recipes cannot include ingredients that are brand-specific.

Entries can be one-dish suppers or dinners, main dishes, side dishes, appetizers or desserts. We encourage supplemental menus and anecdotes about special quick after-work meals and experiences.

Grand prize: $500 cash, a library of Fisher Books cookbooks, plus a pasta machine and a food processor. The winning recipe will be published in a future *Quick After-Work* cookbook.

Second prize: $200 cash, a library of Fisher Books cookbooks, a pasta machine and a food processor.

Purchase is not required for entry. One entry per person. Entries will be judged by Helen Fisher and a panel of cookbook authors and Fisher Books editors. Winners will be required to sign a publicity release and a certificate of eligibility and to give permission to reprint the recipe in various media. All recipes become the property of Fisher Books and will not be returned. The contestant's name, address and phone number must be submitted with the recipe.

Mail your entry to: Quick After-Work Recipe Contest
4239 W. Ina Road, #101
Tucson, AZ 85741

Name _____

Address _____

City/State/ZIP _____

Phone _____

Store where book was purchased _____

Entries must be postmarked by August 31, 1996.